"With the renewed quest for a deeper spirituality and a sense of prayer at all levels of the church's life....Ms. Hintz captures the spirit of this renewal in a practical and helpful way."

David Norris
Catholic Campus Ministry Assn.

"...sourcebook of prayer services in the local church adaptable enough to permit spontaneity."

Martha Radsick
*Christian Bookseller*

"Recommended as a helpful resource for local church organizations, educators, and worship committees."

*National Bulletin on Liturgy*
Ottawa, Canada

"Whether put to use 'as is' or as a model, these prayers can be a positive contribution to the quality of parish life and the work of the church."

*Columba*

"...creative prayer celebrations that can be used at various small group gatherings in the church community. Every committee would profit from the experience of these prayers....Content has a sound scriptural basis and is highly recommended."

Sr. Jean Ackerman
*Common Sense*

"...will be a big help, especially for those who hold the ideal of building a service around the Scriptures but cannot always manage the time to locate and select desirable passages."

Sharon M. Guevin
*Church Teachers*

"...helps small or large group sessions in a prayerful manner appropriate to the season of the year."

National Federation of
Christian Life Communities

"...appropriate for setting the tone and prayerful environment for various meetings and gatherings."

*Aids in Ministry*

"Prayer services weren't even mentioned in my seminary days, so this practical volume fills a real need."

Rev. Charles Dollen
*The Priest*

"Debra Hintz has provided a valuable tool for leaders who would like to present the local church's 'work at hand' as the work of the people of God."

*Religious Education*

# Prayer Services

for

# Parish Meetings

Debra Hintz

△ TWENTY-THIRD PUBLICATIONS

Mystic, Connecticut

# Acknowledgments

Scripture texts used in this work are excerpted from *The Jerusalem Bible*, copyright © 1966 by Darton, Longman & Todd, Ltd. and Doubleday & Company, Inc. Used by permission of the publisher.

Excerpts from the English translation of *The Roman Missal* copyright © 1973, International Committee on English in the Liturgy, Inc. All rights reserved.

"Monday, February 19" from *A cry for Mercy: Prayers from the Genesee* by Henri J.M. Nouwen, copyright © 1981 by Doubleday & Company, Inc. Used by permission of the publisher.

Excerpts of "Jesus Bears His Cross" and "The Hospital" from *Prayers* by Michel Quoist, copyright © 1963 by Sheed and Ward.

"Hidden God" and "Suspice" from *God of Seasons* by Michael E. Moynahan, S.J., copyright © 1980 by Resource Publications, Inc. Used with permission.

Excerpt from *Prayers for the Domestic Church: A Handbook for Worship in the Home* by Rev. Edward M. Hays, copyright © 1979 by Forest of Peace Books, Inc., Easton, KS 66020. Reprinted with permission.

"Psalm 51" and "Psalm 33" from *The Psalms* by Bonaventure Zerr, O.S.B., copyright © 1979 by Paulist Press. Used by permission of Paulist Press.

"Romans 12" and "Philemon" from *Epistles/Now* by Leslie F. Brandt, copyright © 1974 by Concordia Publishing House. Reprinted with permission.

Excerpt from *Walking on the Wings of the Wind* by Archbishop Rembert G. Weakland, O.S.B., copyright © 1980 by Paulist Press. Used by permission of Paulist Press.

Also included are the works of several other authors and sources. When known, the author or source is recognized within the text. Their contributions to this work are greatly appreciated.

Gratitude is also given to the people of St. Margaret Mary Parish Community, Milwaukee, who have prayed and inspired many of these prayers in the abundant gatherings of parish life.

**Seventh printing 1991**

Twenty-Third Publications
185 Willow Street
P.O. Box 180
Mystic, CT 06355
(203) 536-2611

ISBN 0-89622-170-9
Library of Congress Catalog Card Number 83-70620

Art by Debra Hintz

## DEDICATION

For a very special man
who has touched my life and my ministry
with love and support

and my grandmother, Angela,
whose life of love, simplicity, and great faith
will always be a very rich and beautiful influence
in my life.

# Contents

Introduction   1

Gathering Prayer   4

In the Assembly of Your People   6

Morning Prayer   8

Evening Prayer   10

Waiting   12

Christmas   16

Lenten Prayer   18

Lord, By Your Cross   20

He Is Risen!   22

Spring Prayer   24

Summer   26

September Prayer   29

Autumn Prayer   30

Winter Prayer   32

Bread from the Earth, Wine to Gladden Hearts   34

The Breaking of Bread   36

Reconciled   38

Come Back to Me with All Your Heart   40

Compassion and Mercy   42

The Gift We Offer      44

In Your Name      46

A Light to All Nations      50

The Breath of God in Us      52

Announce the Good News      54

Beginning      56

Sing Glory to God      58

In Thanksgiving      60

The Spirit Among Us      62

Prayer for Unity      65

Dream Dreams      66

Live Simply      68

Prayer in Times of Decision Making      70

The New and Unknown      72

Prayer in Times of Frustration and Doubt      74

Prayer in Times of Illness      76

I Go to Prepare a Place for You      78

Celebration! Prayer When Work is Completed      80

Parting      83

Leave-Taking      84

As We Go Forth      86

# Introduction

Anyone involved in the ministry of the church is familiar with the many gatherings necessary in community life. We gather as staffs, committees, faculties, study groups, boards, organizations, and families—in a word, as communities of believers. We come together in churches, libraries, schools, halls, rectories, and homes; we come together for meetings, conferences, presentations, and celebrations. As we enter a gathering we exchange smiles, waves, and enter into conversations. We recognize the presence of one another.

But what about the presence of the Father, the Lord Jesus, and the Spirit? God is in our midst when we gather in his name. When we gather, do we welcome the Lord as we have those around us? Do we take the time to say, "Be among us, guide us, give us strength, open our minds, touch our hearts, and show us your love"? Do we recognize that the work before us is the work of the Lord? Do we give thanksgiving for the good given us? Who else will counsel us, strengthen and guide us, care for us, give us wisdom? Without that presence, is not our gathering for naught?

How many times do we neglect to pray with these communities before we begin our work? How many times do we pray "quickly" because no one was able to take the time to prepare? This isn't unusual in our hurried society.

The gathering prayers of this book are celebrations of God's presence. They are celebrations of joy and glory, seasons, gifts and talents, forgiveness and healing, thanksgiving, comings and goings, beginnings and endings. All of these are part of our lives in the community of God's people.

*Prayer Services for Parish Meetings* provides those who gather the opportunity to spend time in prayer and celebration. These prayer sessions are structured to involve all the people in song, scripture, and prayer. Yet, the songs, reflection periods, meditations, and the time for spontaneous prayer are flexible, allowing each group to make these elements even more appropriate and meaningful for their gathering.

As you gather with your community, make these prayers your own. Add your songs, pray your prayers, and recognize the Lord's presence in his word and in your response, for he is among you in your gathering.

*Selecting
A Prayer
Service*

When choosing a prayer, pay special attention to the type of gathering, the theme of your celebration, topics on your agenda, and the time of year. Look at the prayers carefully and make sure the one you choose is relevant in some way to your gathering.

*Preparation*

Those who lead prayer always need to prepare the service. Even though these services may be easy to follow, you need to be familiar with each one before praying. Music needs to be chosen, leaders and readers need to prepare their readings, and the environment needs to be set. All this should be done before the prayer service begins, so that all will enter into the experience and be touched by it.

Another key to a prayer service that flows is to prepare the people with any instructions before prayer begins. Make these as simple as possible, however. For example, if a psalm response is divided "left" and "right," let everyone know beforehand who is "left" and who is "right." Do not interrupt prayer to suddenly explain something. You may also want to explain or announce music selections beforehand.

It is also important to have a period of silence before a prayer service in order to allow the people to prepare, placing themselves in God's presence and setting their hearts and minds on prayer.

*Scripture
Readings*

The texts of scripture readings, except when read by all the people, are not included in these prayer services, since the Word is more appropriately read from a book of scripture. This also gives the people the opportunity to listen to the reading as it is proclaimed. Readers should be asked to prepare their parts in advance.

*Music*

Suggestions for music have not been included in this book, although "Opening Song" and "Closing Song" have been indicated in some of the prayers. The type of music and specific songs used by different communities varies greatly. Each group should decide on the songs they think would best fit the prayer theme. Music can also be used where "Meditation" and "Reflection" are indicated, as well as in places where music is not suggested.

*Setting*    Even if you are coming together for a meeting, a special environment for prayer can still be achieved. Set a mood for prayer. Lights can be dimmed, a single candle lit, and background music played as people gather before prayer begins.

*Creativity*    When preparing a prayer service, use your creativity. The prayer will then become yours. If you feel you would like to use music where it is not indicated, do so. You might prefer to sing the psalm response. Or replace it with a song. Audiovisual materials can also be used. Slides, filmstrips, and movies can enhance prayer. Slides, for instance, can be used to illustrate a reading. A single slide projected during the entire prayer can help set a mood. Filmstrips and brief movies can be used in place of a reading. The use of light, water, oil, and other symbols can add another dimension to prayer.

*Spontaneous Prayer*    Times for "Spontaneous Prayer" are indicated in some of the services. Spontaneous prayer can be in the form of general intercessions, in which case the leader should announce a response such as "Lord, hear our prayer" or "Hear us, O Lord." Or this can be a time for people to simply pray their own prayer in silence. Not everyone feels comfortable expressing their prayers publicly. This should be respected.

*Reflections and Meditations*    "Reflection" and "Meditation" have also been indicated in many of the prayers. These can be silent times. Music can also be used. In these cases it can be instrumental or sung, recorded or live. You may like to use a reading, depending on where the reflection or meditation is located in the prayer.

*Note On Use of Language:* Throughout this book, God is often referred to in the masculine gender. Recognizing the sensitivities of people, you are encouraged in reading these prayers to change to a neutral or feminine gender if you so desire. The same is true in scripture passages and other readings where the masculine language was part of the original texts and, in accordance with copyright agreements, was required to be copied verbatim.

3

# Gathering Prayer

OPENING SONG

**Leader**  Lord, from age to age you gather a people to yourself, so that from East to West a perfect offering may be made to the glory of your name.

**All**  In the presence of this assembly, Lord, we give you thanks and praise.

**Leader**  Be with us in this gathering, Lord. Make us one as we proclaim your wondrous deeds and magnificent love.

**All**  We ask this in the name of our Lord Jesus Christ, who lives and reigns forever. Amen.

**Reader**  Isaiah 43:1-10

SILENT REFLECTION

*Psalm Response*

**Left**  Then I shall proclaim your name to my brothers and sisters,
praise you in full assembly:
you who fear Yahweh, praise him!
Entire race of Jacob, glorify him!
Entire race of Israel, revere him!

**Right**  You are the theme of my praise in the Great Assembly,
I perform my vows in the presence of those who fear him.
The poor will receive as much as they want to eat.
Those who seek Yahweh will praise him.
Long life to their hearts!

**Left**  The whole earth, from end to end, will remember
and come back to Yahweh;
all the families of the nations will bow down before him.
For Yahweh reigns, the ruler of nations!

**Right**  Before him all the prosperous of the earth will bow down,
before him will bow all who go down to the dust.
And my soul will live for him.

**All**  My children will serve him;
people will proclaim the Lord to generations still to come,
his righteousness to a people yet unborn.
All this he has done.  *Psalm 22*

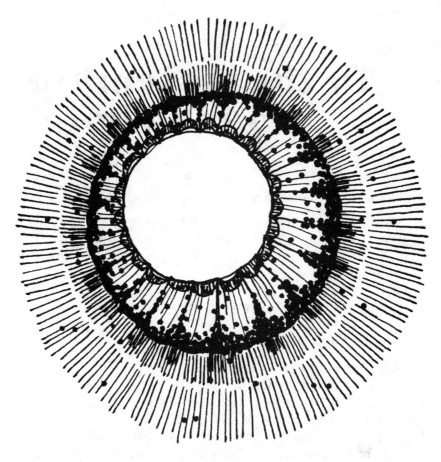

**Leader** Lord God, you are the source of our being, the grantor of our prayers. Hear the needs of your people, for without your love and care we are capable of nothing.

SPONTANEOUS PRAYER

**Leader** Having expressed our needs, let us pray together the words Jesus gave us.

**All** Our Father in heaven,
may your name be held holy,
your kingdom come,
your will be done
on earth as in heaven.
Give us today our daily bread.
And forgive us our debts,
as we have forgiven those who are in debt to us.
And do not put us to the test,
but save us from the evil one.

**Leader** As we gather today, Lord, we reach out to you, our counselor, our light, the Lord of our lives. May the work we are about to share be a reflection of the love you alone can give. May it also be evident at the end of our day that our great love for you was part of this gathering. Let it be known on our faces and in our words that your presence was in our hearts as we came together. We ask this in the name of our Lord, Jesus Christ. Amen.

# In the Assembly of Your People

**Leader**   Come, let us worship the Lord for he is our God and we are his people.

**All**   Be praised, Lord our God and Ruler of the universe, in giving us life, sustaining us, and bringing us to this day. Amen.

OPENING SONG

**Reader**   Ephesians 1:3-6, 11-14

*Psalm Response*

**All**   Acclaim Yahweh, all the earth,
serve Yahweh, gladly,
come into his presence with songs of joy!
Know that he, Yahweh, is God,
he made us and we belong to him,
we are his people, the flock that he pastures.
Walk through his porticoes giving thanks,
enter his courts praising him,
give thanks to him, bless his name!
Yes, Yahweh is good,
his love is everlasting,
his faithfulness endures from age to age. *Psalm 100*

**Reader**   Ephesians 4:1-6

REFLECTION

*Prayers of Petition*

**Reader**   Father, we your children come before you today in need of your undying love and understanding. As we bring ourselves before you, hear our prayers and breathe new life into us that we may show your greatness to all.

We ask that each of us finds your Spirit within us today, that we may celebrate Christ with all our being.

*All*   Father, awaken your Spirit in us.

*Reader*   We ask that our community rejoice in the goodness and love your Son's coming brings.

*All*   Father, open our minds and our hearts.

*Reader*   We ask that we may be able to take the joy and love we celebrate here to others who live among us.

*All*   Father, be with us.

*Reader*   And Father, we ask too that the world may be open to you, that peace may reign, and that your love and your word may someday find no barriers.

*All*   Father, bring us peace.

*Reader*   We ask, Father, that you be with us always, that you love and guide us, bring us through times both happy and sad, that you never forsake us even as we fail or as we turn from you; for you are our God and we are your people.

*All*   Amen.

*Leader*   The Lord is our God and we are his people. As a community of believers and as a celebrating people, let us join together saying . . .

*All*   Our Father . . .

*Leader*   The grace of our Lord Jesus Christ, the love of God, and the fellowship of the Holy Spirit be with you all!

*All*   And also with you.

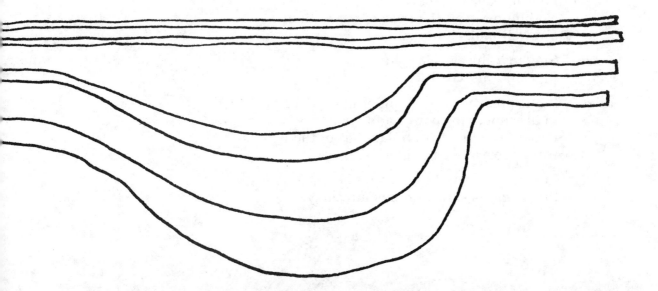

# Morning Prayer

*Leader*    Praise Yahweh, all nations,
        extol him, all you peoples!

*All*    For his love is strong,
        his faithfulness eternal.    *Psalm 117*

OPENING MEDITATION

*Leader*    Father, as we gather our tired bodies this morning, we remind ourselves of your love. Let our minds and hearts once again be awakened today. May our enthusiasm and joy be seen in our eyes that others may follow. Let our entire being proclaim your greatness, and let your love touch others today through our lives. We ask this through Jesus Christ, our Lord and brother. Amen.

*Reader*    Ephesians 1:15-19

*Psalm Response:*

*Reader*    Sing to Yahweh, bless his name.
    Proclaim his salvation day after day.

*All*    Sing to Yahweh, bless his name.
    Proclaim his salvation day after day.

*Reader*    Sing Yahweh a new song!
    Sing to Yahweh, all the earth!
    Tell of his glory among the nations,
    tell his marvels to every people.

*All*    Sing to Yahweh, bless his name.
    Proclaim his salvation day after day.

*Reader*    Yahweh is great, loud must be his praise,
    he is to be feared beyond all gods.
    Nothingness, all the gods of the nations.
    Yahweh himself made the heavens.

*All*    Sing to Yahweh, bless his name.
    Proclaim his salvation day after day.

*Reader*    In his presence are splendor and majesty,
    in his sanctuary power and beauty.
    Pay tribute to Yahweh, families of the peoples,
    tribute to Yahweh of glory and power.

*All*    Sing to Yahweh, bless his name.
    Proclaim his salvation day after day.

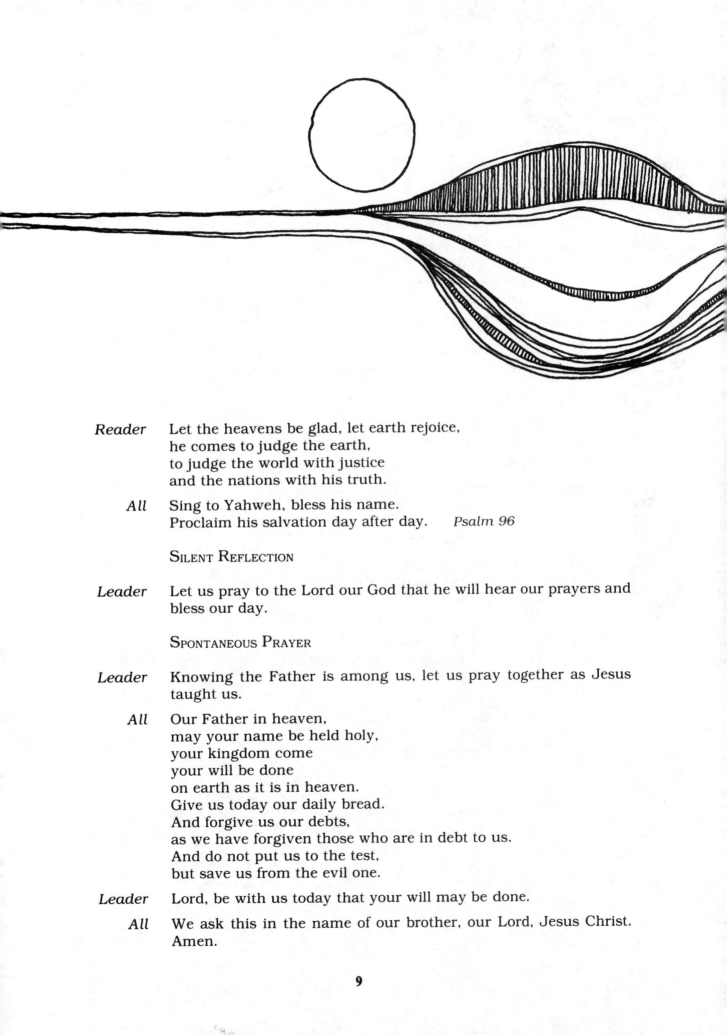

Reader    Let the heavens be glad, let earth rejoice,
he comes to judge the earth,
to judge the world with justice
and the nations with his truth.

All    Sing to Yahweh, bless his name.
Proclaim his salvation day after day.    *Psalm 96*

SILENT REFLECTION

Leader    Let us pray to the Lord our God that he will hear our prayers and
bless our day.

SPONTANEOUS PRAYER

Leader    Knowing the Father is among us, let us pray together as Jesus
taught us.

All    Our Father in heaven,
may your name be held holy,
your kingdom come
your will be done
on earth as it is in heaven.
Give us today our daily bread.
And forgive us our debts,
as we have forgiven those who are in debt to us.
And do not put us to the test,
but save us from the evil one.

Leader    Lord, be with us today that your will may be done.

All    We ask this in the name of our brother, our Lord, Jesus Christ.
Amen.

# Evening Prayer

**Leader**  Lord, be with us tonight as the sun sets on our day.

**All**  Come, bless Yahweh,
all you who serve Yahweh,
serving in the house of Yahweh,
in the courts of the house of our God!
Stretch out your hands toward the sanctuary,
bless Yahweh night after night!
May Yahweh bless you from Zion,
he who made heaven and earth!    *Psalm 134*

OPENING MEDITATION

*Psalm Prayer*

**Left**  You servants of Yahweh, praise,
praise the name of Yahweh!
Blessed be the name of Yahweh,
henceforth and for ever!

**Right**  From east to west,
praised be the name of Yahweh!
High over all nations, Yahweh!
His glory transcends the heavens!

**Left**  Who is like Yahweh our God?
enthroned so high, he needs to stoop
to see the sky and earth!

**Right**  He raises the poor from the dust;
he lifts the needy from the dunghill
to give them a place with princes,
with the princes of his people.

| *All* | You servants of Yahweh, praise,<br>praise the name of Yahweh!<br>Blessed be the name of Yahweh,<br>henceforth and for ever!<br>From east to west,<br>praised be the name of Yahweh! *from Psalm 113* |

*Reader*   Ephesians 5:8-21

*Psalm Response*

| *Right* | It is good to give thanks to Yahweh,<br>to play in honor of your name, Most High, |
| *Left* | To proclaim your love at daybreak<br>and your faithfulness all through the night |
| *Right* | To the music of the zither and lyre,<br>to the rippling of the harp. |
| *Left* | I am happy, Yahweh, at what you have done;<br>at your achievements I joyfully exclaim,<br>"Great are your achievements, Yahweh,<br>immensely deep your thoughts!" *from Psalm 92* |

SILENT REFLECTION

*Leader*   Let us pray.

*All*   Our Father . . .

*Leader*   Lord, protect us throughout the night that we may rise again in the morning to sing your praises. Grant us peace and tranquility in our rest, love and strength in the new day. We ask this through Jesus Christ, our Lord and brother. Amen.

# Waiting

OPENING MEDITATION

**Leader**    Lord, we await your coming during this season of anticipation. Fill our lives with your presence. Fulfill our hopes and our dreams. Let your light break through our darkness as we announce the coming of Immanuel, God with us. Be with us, Lord, as we ready ourselves.

**Reader**    Isaiah 40:3-5,9-11

*Psalm Response*

**Reader**    Let Yahweh enter; he is king of glory.

**All**    Let Yahweh enter; he is king of glory.

**Reader**    To Yahweh belong earth and all it holds,
the world and all who live in it;
he himself founded it on the ocean,
based it firmly on the nether sea.

**All**    Let Yahweh enter; he is king of glory.

**Reader**    Who has the right to climb the mountain of Yahweh,
who the right to stand in his holy place?
He whose hands are clean, whose heart is pure,
whose soul does not pay homage to worthless things
and who never swears to a lie.

**All**    Let Yahweh enter; he is king of glory.

**Reader**    The blessing of Yahweh is his,
and vindication from God his savior.
Such are the people who seek him,
who seek your presence, God of Jacob!

**All**    Let Yahweh enter; he is king of glory.    *from Psalm 24*

**Reader**    Isaiah 11:1-10

*waiting*

*Psalm Response*

**Right**  God, give your own justice to the king,
     your own righteousness to the royal son,
so that he may rule your people rightly
     and your poor with justice.

**Left**  Let the mountains and hills
     bring a message of peace for the people.
Uprightly he will defend the poorest,
he will save the children of those in need,
     and crush their oppressors.

**Right**  In his days virtue will flourish,
     a universal peace till the moon is no more;
his empire shall stretch from sea to sea,
     from the river to the ends of the earth.

**Left**  Blessed be his name for ever,
     enduring as long as the sun!
May every race in the world be blessed in him,
     and all the nations call him blessed!  *from Psalm 72*

**Reader**  Isaiah 9:1-6

*Shared Response*

**Reader**  Cry out with joy and gladness:
for among you is the great and Holy One of Israel.

**All**  Cry out with joy and gladness:
for among you is the great and Holy One of Israel.

**Reader**  See now, he is the God of my salvation.
I have trust now and no fear,
for Yahweh is my strength, my song,
he is my salvation.
And you will draw water joyfully
from the springs of salvation.

*waiting*

|          |                                                                                                                                                                                                        |
| -------- | ------------------------------------------------------------------------------------------------------------------------------------------------------------------------------------------------------ |
| *All*    | Cry out with joy and gladness:<br>for among you is the great and Holy One of Israel.                                                                                                                   |
| *Reader* | That day, you will say:<br>Give thanks to Yahweh,<br>call his name aloud.<br>Proclaim his deeds to the people,<br>declare his name sublime.                                                            |
| *All*    | Cry out with joy and gladness:<br>for among you is the great and Holy One of Israel.                                                                                                                   |
| *Reader* | Sing of Yahweh, for he has done marvelous things,<br>let them be made known to the whole world.<br>Cry out for joy and gladness,<br>you dwellers in Zion,<br>for great in the midst of you<br>is the Holy One of Israel. |
| *All*    | Cry out with joy and gladness:<br>for among you is the great and Holy One of Israel.          *Isaiah 12:2-6*                                                                                          |

SILENT REFLECTION

| *Leader* | Let us pray. |

SPONTANEOUS PRAYER

| *Leader* | We believe that the Son of God once came to us.<br>We look for him to come again.<br>May his coming bring us the light of his holiness<br>And free us with his blessings. |
| *All*    | Amen. |

*waiting*

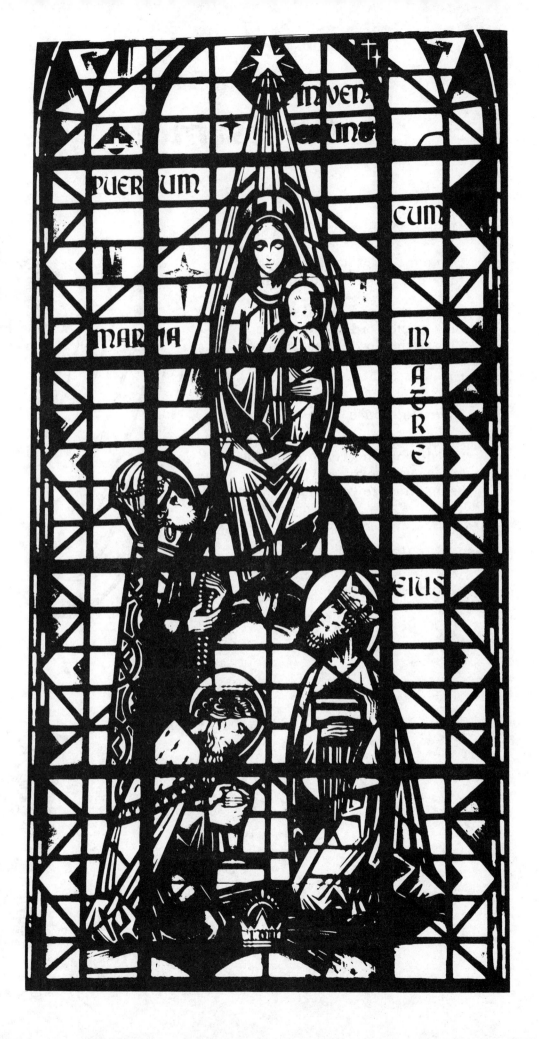

# Christmas

OPENING MEDITATION

Leader    God our Father has sent his Son
to be our light and salvation.

All    Sing to the Lord a new song;
Sing to the Lord, all you lands.
Sing to the Lord, bless his name.

Reader    Isaiah 9:1-6

*Psalm Response*

All    I thank you, Yahweh, with all my heart;
I recite your marvels one by one,
I rejoice and exult in you,
I sing praise to your name, Most High.
*from Psalm 9*

Reader    John 1:1-5, 9-14

SONG RESPONSE

*Prayer of Praise*

*All*  Sing Yahweh a new song!
Sing to Yahweh, all the earth!
Sing to Yahweh, bless his name.
Proclaim his salvation day after day,
tell of his glory among
　　the nations,
tell his marvels
　　to every people.
Yahweh is great,
　　loud must be his praise,
he is to be feared
　　beyond all gods.
Nothingness, all the gods
　　of the nations.
Yahweh himself made
　　the heavens,
in his presence are
　　splendor and majesty,
in his sanctuary
　　power and beauty.
Pay tribute to Yahweh,
　　families of the peoples,
tribute to Yahweh
　　of glory and power,
tribute to Yahweh
　　of his name's due glory.　　*from Psalm 96*

CLOSING SONG

# *Lenten Prayer*

OPENING MEDITATION

Leader     Father, we are a sinful people. We have run from you and have rejected your ways. We are distracted at times. We are weak and doubtful. Yet your love is always present, always unconditional. We are on our way back to you, Lord. Be at our side.

Reader     Jeremiah 13:15-17

*Psalm Response*

Reader     Be good to me, Yahweh, and hear my prayer.

All     Be good to me, Yahweh, and hear my prayer.

Reader     God, guardian of my rights, you answer when I call,
when I am in trouble, you come to my relief:
now be good to me and hear my prayer.

All     Be good to me, Yahweh, and hear my prayer.

Reader     You men, why shut your hearts so long,
loving delusions, chasing after lies?
Know this, Yahweh works wonders for those he loves,
Yahweh hears me when I call to him.

All     Be good to me, Yahweh, and hear my prayer.

Reader     Tremble: give up sinning,
spend your night in quiet meditation.
Offer sacrifice in a right spirit, and trust Yahweh.

All     Be good to me, Yahweh, and hear my prayer.

Reader     "Who will give us sight of happiness?" many say.
Show us the light of your face, turned toward us!
Yahweh, you have given more joy to my heart
than others ever know, for all their corn and wine.

All     Be good to me, Yahweh, and hear my prayer.

Reader     In peace I lie down, and fall asleep at once,
since you alone, Yahweh, make me rest secure.

All     Be good to me, Yahweh, and hear my prayer.     *Psalm 4*

Reader     Why, O Lord, is it so hard for me to keep my heart directed toward you? Why do the many little things I want to do, and the many people I know, keep crowding my mind, even during the hours that I am totally free to be with you and you alone? Why does my mind wander off in so many directions, and why does my heart desire the things that lead me astray? Are you not enough for me? Do I keep doubting your love and care, your mercy and grace? Do I keep wondering, in the center of my being, whether you will give me all I need if I just keep my eyes on you?

Please accept my distractions, my fatigue, my irritations, and my faithless wanderings. You know me more deeply and fully than I know myself. You love me with a greater love than I can love myself. You even offer me more than I can desire. Look at me, see me in all my misery and inner confusion, and let me sense your presence in the midst of my turmoil. All I can do is show myself to you. Yet, I am afraid to do so. I am afraid that you will reject me. But I know—with the knowledge of faith—that you desire to give me your love. The only thing you ask of me is not to hide from you, not to run away in despair, not to act as if you were a relentless despot.

Take my tired body, my confused mind, and my restless soul into your arms and give me rest, simple quiet rest. Do I ask too much too soon? I should not worry about that. You will let me know. Come, Lord Jesus, come. Amen.    *Monday, February 19, A Cry for Mercy*, Henri J.M. Nouwen

SILENT REFLECTION

*Reader*    Matthew 16:24-28

SILENT REFLECTION

*Leader*    Let us pray.

SPONTANEOUS PRAYER

*Leader*    Father, hear the prayers of your people. Lead us back to you that we may continue the work of your Son. We ask this through Jesus Christ, our Lord and Savior.

*All*    Amen.

LENTEN Prayer

# *Lord, By Your Cross...*

*Leader*    Lord, by the suffering of Christ your Son you have saved us all from the death we inherited from sinful Adam. By the law of nature we have borne the likeness of his manhood. May the sanctifying power of grace help us to put on the likeness of our Lord in heaven, who lives and reigns forever and ever. Amen.    *Good Friday Services*

*Reader*    Matthew 16:24-28

SILENT REFLECTION

*All*    Lord, I accept my cross, but with hesitation. Why do I choose to leave my comfortable world and allow hardship and pain into my life? I bear it that others may know you more fully through me. Be at my side as I begin my journey. Give me strength and courage.

*Reader*    Luke 23:18-24

SILENT REFLECTION

*All*    And yet ours were the sufferings he bore, ours the sorrows he carried. But we, we thought of him as someone punished, struck by God, and brought low. Yet he was pierced through for our faults, crushed for our sins. On him lies a punishment that brings us peace, and through his wounds we are healed.    *Isaiah 53:4-5*

*Reader*    John 19:16-19

S<small>ILENT</small> R<small>EFLECTION</small>

*Response*

*All*    Lord, here is your cross. Your cross. As if it were your cross. You had no cross and you came to get ours and all through your life, and along the way to Calvary, you took upon you, one by one, the sins of the world. You have to go forward, and bend, and suffer. The cross must be carried.

Lord, I would rather fight the cross; to bear it is hard. The more I progress, and the more I see the evil in the world, the heavier is the cross on my shoulders. Lord, help me understand that the most generous deed is nothing unless it is also silently redemptive. And since you want for me this long way of the cross, at the dawning of each day, help me to set forth.    *Jesus Bears His Cross, Prayers,*
Michel Quoist

*Leader*    Lord, send down your abundant blessing upon us, your people, who have devoutly recalled the death of your son in the hope of the Resurrection. Grant us pardon and bring us comfort. May our faith grow stronger and our eternal salvation be assured. We ask this through Christ our Lord. Amen.    *Good Friday Services*

# He Is Risen!

| | |
|---|---|
| *Leader* | Be glad my sisters and brothers! The Lord Jesus has risen from the dead! |
| *All* | Let us rejoice in the great love he has shown. |
| *Leader* | May his gracious peace be with you. |
| *All* | And also with you. |
| *Reader* | Matthew 28:1-6 |

SILENT REFLECTION

| | |
|---|---|
| *Reader* | Luke 24:13-35 |
| *Right* | In the grave they laid him, love by hatred slain. Thinking that he would never awake again. Laid in the earth like grain that sleeps unseen. Love is come again like wheat that springs up green. |
| *Left* | Forth he came at Easter like the risen grain. Jesus, who for three days in the grave has lain. Live from dead our risen Lord is seen. Love is come again like wheat that springs up green. |
| *Right* | When our hearts are wintry, grieving or in pain, your dear touch can call them back to life again. Fields of our hearts that dead and bare have been. Love is come again like wheat that springs up green. |
| *Left* | Now the green blade rises from the buried grain. Wheat that in the dark earth many days has lain. Love lives again that with the dead has been. Love is come again like wheat that springs up green. *John M.C. Crum* |

SILENT REFLECTION

| | |
|---|---|
| *Leader* | Sing Alleluia! Give glory to our Lord Jesus Christ. |
| *All* | Alleluia! |
| *Leader* | Christ is risen and makes all things new. |
| *All* | Alleluia! |
| *Leader* | He has been raised never to die again. |
| *All* | Alleluia! |

# Spring Prayer

Opening Meditation

**Leader**    Let us pray. Father, this season brings with it signs of your over-whelming love. The warmth of the sun, the soft gentle rains and the new life coming forth are all beautiful reminders of your life-giving love and compassion. Let us, too, be awakened this spring that we, like all your creation, may be a reflection of you.

**Reader**    Genesis 2:4b-7

*Psalm Response*

**Left**    Let heaven praise Yahweh:
praise him, heavenly heights,
praise him, all his angels,
praise him, all his armies!

**Right**    Praise him, sun and moon,
praise him, shining stars,
praise him, highest heavens,
and waters above the heavens!

**Left**    Let them all praise the name of Yahweh,
at whose command they were created;
he has fixed them in their places for ever,
by an unalterable statute.

**Right**    Let earth praise Yahweh:
sea monsters and all the deeps,
fire and hail, snow and mist,
gales that obey his decree

*Left*    Mountains and hills,
orchards and forests,
wild animals and farm animals,
snakes and birds.

*All*    All kings on earth and nations,
princes, all rulers in the world,
young men and girls,
old people, and children too!
Let them all praise the name of Yahweh,
for his name and no other is sublime,
transcending earth and heaven in majesty,
raising the fortunes of his people,
to the praises of the devout,
of Israel, the people dear to him.    *Psalm 148*

*Reader*    Revelation 21:1-5

SONG RESPONSE

*Leader*    Let us give praise and thanksgiving to God our Father.

SPONTANEOUS PRAYER

*Leader*    We give thanks to you, O Lord, for all your gifts. Your beauty has been made known to us through your creations. May we never stop praising your glorious works.

*All*    Glory be to the Father, and to the Son, and to the Holy Spirit. As it was in the beginning, is now, and ever shall be world without end. Amen.

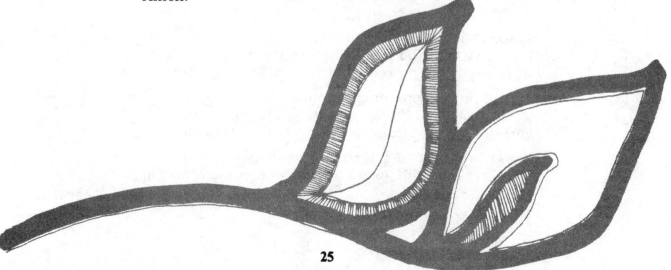

# Summer

Opening Song

**Leader**    Let us pray. Lord God, your warmth and beauty surround us this season. You cleanse and refresh us with the new life you bring. Your wondrous works are signs of your great love. But we have a tendency to neglect you, Lord, as we become engrossed in the activities of the summer months. Be with us. Give us constant reminders of your presence as we promise to always give you praise. We ask this through Jesus Christ, our Lord and brother, who lives and reigns forever. Amen.

*Shared Response*

**All**    O most high, almighty, good Lord God,
to you belong praise, glory, honor, and all blessing.
Praise be my Lord God with all his creatures,
and especially our brother the sun,
who brings us the day and
who brings us the night; fair is he and
shines with a very great splendor;
O Lord, he signifies you to us.

Praise be my Lord for our sister the moon,
and for the stars, which he has set clear
and lovely in the heaven.

Praise be my Lord for our brother the wind,
and for all the air, and clouds, calms and
all weather by which you uphold life in all creatures.

Praised be my Lord for our sister the water,
who is very serviceable to us and humble and
precious and very clean.

Praised be my Lord for our brother fire,
through whom you give us light in the darkness;
he is bright and pleasant and very mighty and strong.

Praised be my Lord for our mother earth,
which sustains us and keeps us, and brings forth
grass and diverse fruits and flowers of many colors.

Praise and bless the Lord, and give thanks to him
and serve him with great humility.    *Canticle of the Sun,*
St. Francis of Assisi

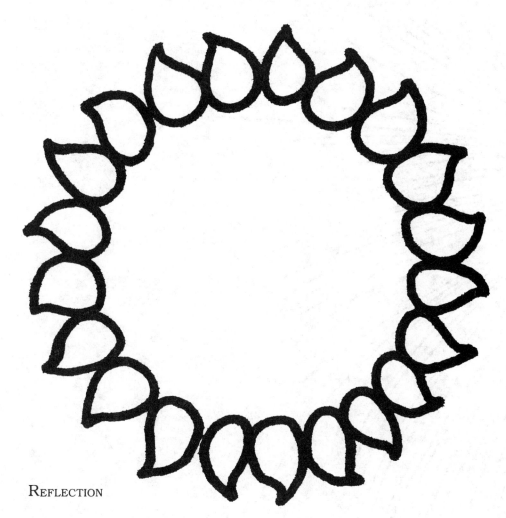

REFLECTION

*Reader*    Psalm 104:1-9, 31-34

REFLECTION

*Leader*    Lord God, you have blessed us with your creation. Still, we are in need of your never-ending care. Hear us now as we pray.

SPONTANEOUS PRAYER

*Leader*    In praise and thanksgiving, let us pray . . .

*All*    Sing to Yahweh in gratitude,
play the lyre for our God:
who covers the heavens with clouds,
to provide the earth with rain,
to produce fresh grass on the hillsides
and the plants that are needed by man,
who gives their food to the cattle
and to the young ravens when they cry.
The strength of the war horse means nothing to him,
it is not infantry that interests him.
Yahweh is interested only in those who fear him,
in those who rely on his love.   *from Psalm 147*

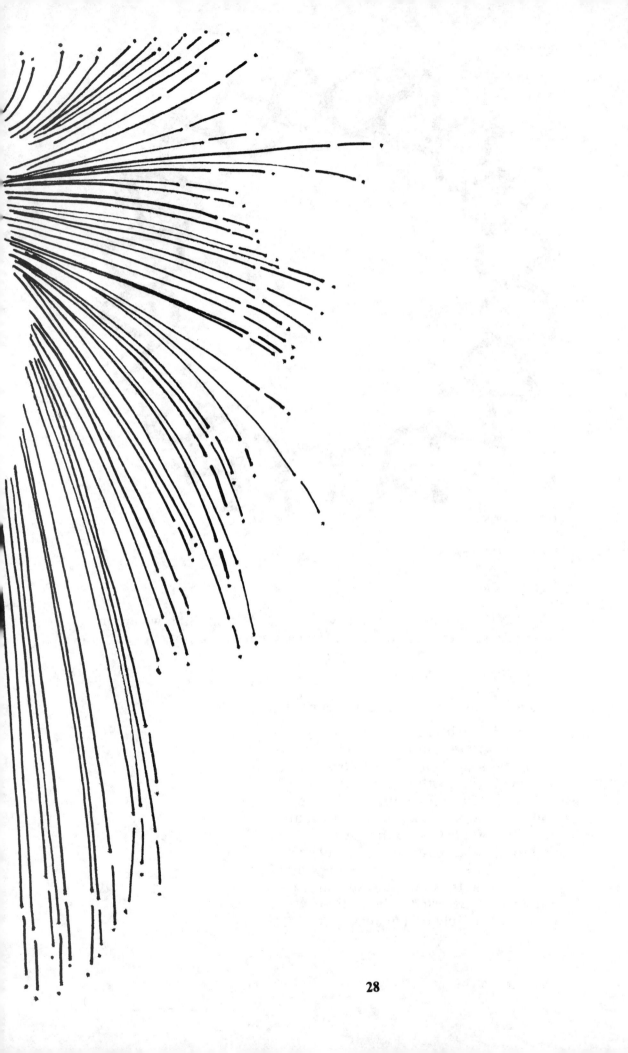

# September Prayer

OPENING SONG

*Leader*  Let us pray. Father, we gather once again as your community of believers as we return from the summer months ready to begin another year. We have been renewed by the slower pace of the past months. Let a new enthusiasm be part of this year. Let the routine and busyness that sometimes cause us to lag be very little in the days ahead. May we be alive in your word. We ask this in the name of Jesus Christ. Amen.

*Reader*  1 Thessalonians 5:12-18

REFLECTION

*Shared Response*

*All*  We pray that our God will make us worthy of his call, and fulfill by his power every honest intention and work of faith. In this way the name of our Lord Jesus may be glorified in us and we in him, in accord with the gracious gift of our God and of the Lord Jesus Christ.

*2 Thessalonians 1:11-12; adapted*

*Leader*  Lord, our God, hear now our hopes and dreams for the coming year.

SPONTANEOUS PRAYER

*Leader*  Let us pray.

*All*  Our Father . . .

*Leader*  May the Lord God grant us constant hope and love that remains forever.

*All*  Amen.

*Leader*  May he strengthen us and bring us peace.

*All*  Amen.

# Autumn Prayer

OPENING MEDITATION

*Leader*   Lord, we come before you in thanksgiving for the gifts you have given. The color of this season reminds us of the beauty you alone can create. We are thankful for the food you provide in the harvest. You have filled the earth with your gifts. You have blessed us. We are ever grateful, Lord, and will never stop singing your praises. To you be honor and glory forever.

*Reader*   Deuteronomy 26:1-11

REFLECTION

*Reader*   Sirach 16:24-28

REFLECTION

*Leader*   Lord God of all creation, hear the prayers of your people.

SPONTANEOUS PRAYER

*Leader*   Let us pray.

*All*    Our Father in heaven,
        may your name be held holy,
        your kingdom come,
        your will be done
        on earth as it is in heaven.
        Give us today our daily bread.
        And forgive those who are in debt to us.
        And do not put us to the test,
        but save us from the evil one.

*All*    May the name of God
        be blessed for ever and for ever,
        since wisdom and power are his alone.
        His, to control the procession of times and seasons,
        to make and unmake kings,
        to confer wisdom on the wise,
        and knowledge on those with wit to discern;
        his to uncover depths and mysteries,
        to know what lies in darkness;
        and light dwells with him.
        To you, God of my fathers, I give thanks and praise.

*Daniel 2:20-23*

# *Winter Prayer*

**Leader**    The love, warmth and peace of the Lord Jesus Christ be with you all.

**All**    And also with you.

**Leader**    Lord, it is sometimes hard to celebrate at this time of the year. It is a cold, dead, barren season. The life and color that were here a few months ago have left us. We long for the warmth of the seasons to come. Help us to remember, Lord, even in the midst of this life-less time, that you still live; that, unlike the season, you still bring life and warmth to our hearts. Let us not forget you, Lord. Send us gentle reminders of your love.

**Reader**    The people of Israel, during a time when they had become "a laughingstock among the peoples" felt the presence of their God was absent and they cried out to him with these words:

Psalm 44:18-27

SILENT REFLECTION

**Reader**    Lord of winter, God of cold, whose presence we are often told is unobtrusive, almost imperceptible, let us catch a passing glimpse of things to come. Enhance our sometimes anxious wait: the painful passage of fear-filled days, worry-weakened winter dreams, chilled delays. Come help us see what frozen eyes are blinded to: the life that slowly comes to be below the surface sight of things

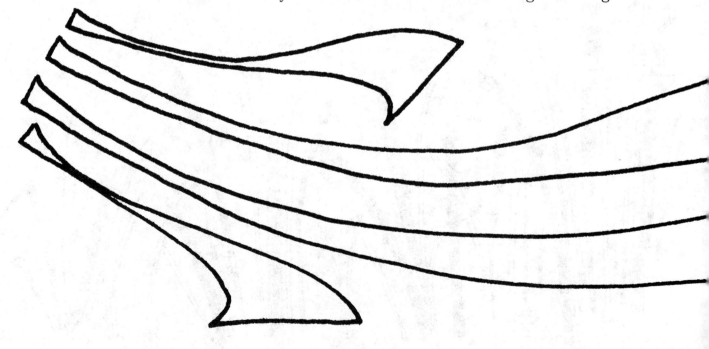

(silent night, quiet life that's cloaked in snow).
O hidden God, you quite confound us with your presence underground. Frost-bitten faith is wearing thin, weak from fasting, looking hard for lasting confirmation of longed comings to be. Lightsome God, send us sun: Your spirit's warming breath. Un-freeze us, ease our doubts, free our frozen faith and icy dreams. Teach us once again your mystery sent in season: a rousing encore of life from death. Come swiftly, quickening Lord. Let winter thaw and gift our hearts with spring.     *Hidden God, God of Seasons,*

Michael E. Moynahan, S.J.

SILENT REFLECTION

*Leader*    Let us pray.

SPONTANEOUS PRAYER

*Leader*    Let us pray to God our Father in the words of Jesus Christ.

*All*    Our Father . . .

*Leader*    May the Lord of life warm our days with his presence.

*All*    Glory be to the Father, and to the Son, and to the Holy Spirit. As it was in the beginning, is now, and ever shall be, world without end. Amen.

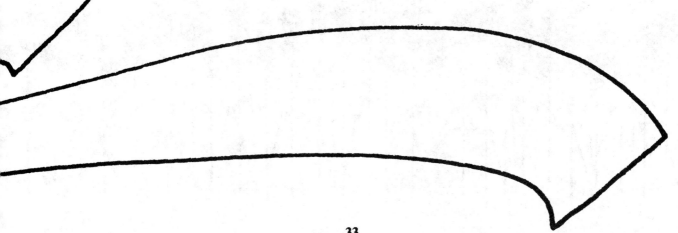

# Bread from the Earth
# Wine to Gladden Hearts

**Leader**    Lord God, you have blessed us with the gifts of your fields, the fruits of the earth. Your love is made known to us in the food that we are about to share. As we come together for this meal, we are grateful for that love. Be with us, Lord, in our celebration.

**Reader**    Bless Yahweh, my soul.
Yahweh, my God, how great you are!
You make fresh grass grow for cattle
and those plants made use of by man,
for them to get food from the soil:
wine to make them cheerful,
oil to make them happy
and bread to make them strong.
All creatures depend on you
to feed them throughout the year;
you provide the food they eat,
with generous hand you satisfy their hunger.
Glory for ever to Yahweh!
May Yahweh find joy in what he creates.
I mean to sing to Yahweh all my life,
I mean to play for my God as long as I live.    *from Psalm 104*

REFLECTION

*Prayer of Praise and Thanksgiving*

**Reader**    In thanksgiving for this meal before us, prepared with the gifts of your love . . .

**All**    We praise you, O Lord.

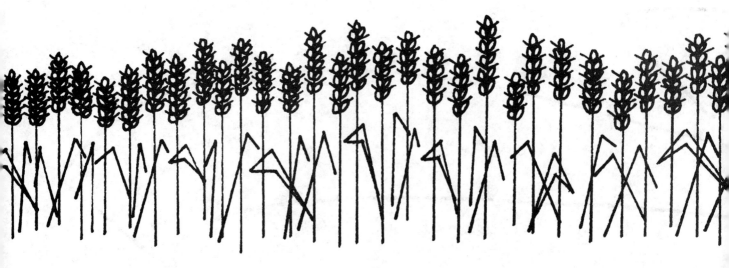

| | |
|---|---|
| *Reader* | For the fields and the animals that bring us our food . . . |
| *All* | We give you thanks. |
| *Reader* | That we may work to feed the hungry and the oppressed of the world . . . |
| *All* | Lord, help us share the blessings you have given. |
| *Reader* | For the nourishment you give in your Word and through your Spirit . . . |
| *All* | We are ever grateful, Lord. |
| *Reader* | For the blessings given through this sharing today . . . |
| *All* | Lord, we give you thanks and praise. |
| *All* | Lord God and Giver of all Good Gifts, |

*All*  Lord God and Giver of all Good Gifts,
   we are grateful as we pause before this meal,
   for all the Blessings of Life that You give to us.
Daily, we are fed with good things,
   nourished by friendship and care,
   feasted with forgiveness and understanding.
And so, mindful of Your Continuous Care,
   we pause to be grateful
   for the blessings of this table.
May Your Presence
   be the "extra" taste to this meal
   which we eat in the name of Your Son, Jesus.

Amen.     *Prayers for the Domestic Church*, Edward M. Hays

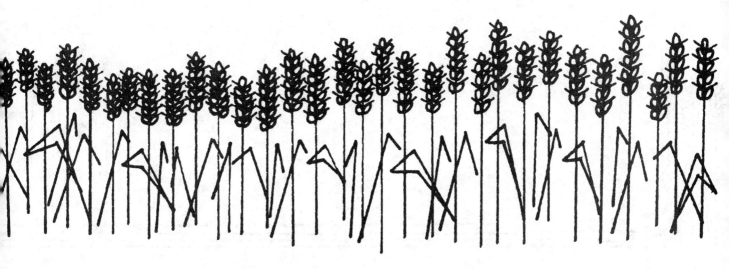

# *The Breaking of Bread*

OPENING MEDITATION

*Leader*    The initial act of a Jewish meal is the breaking of bread. The early Christians shared this tradition in their homes. It was a sign of community. Today, we too, will break bread and share it with one another before our meal, remembering we are community. "Because the loaf of bread is one, we, many though we are, are one body, for we partake of the one loaf."

*Reader*    Acts 2:42-47

REFLECTION

*Reader*    1 Corinthians 10:16-17

REFLECTION

BLESSING OF BREAD AND WINE

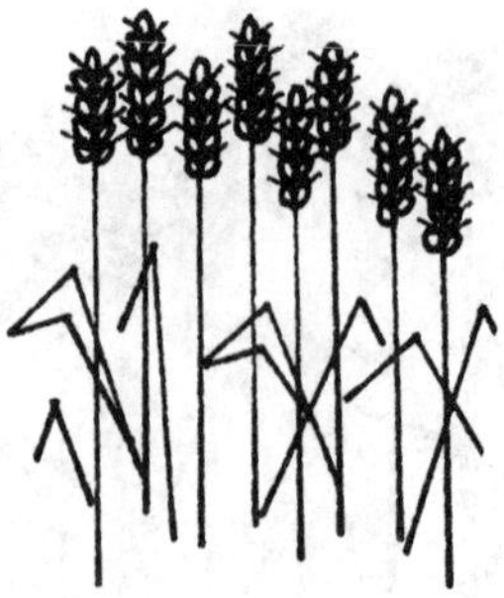

*Leader*  Lord God, through your goodness we have these gifts of bread and wine before us. May your blessing come upon all who share in this meal. May this bread and wine be blessed that as we share them they become symbols of our oneness with you. We ask this in the name of our Lord Jesus Christ. Amen.

Sʜᴀʀɪɴɢ ᴏꜰ Bʀᴇᴀᴅ ᴀɴᴅ Wɪɴᴇ (Share your bread and wine.)

*Leader*  Let us pray.

*All*  Blessed are you, O Lord our God, eternal King, who feeds the whole world with your goodness, with grace, with loving kindness and with tender mercy. You give food to all flesh, for your loving kindness endures forever. Through your great goodness, food has never failed us. O may it not fail us forever, for your name's sake, since you nourish and sustain all living things and do good to all, and provide food for all your creatures whom you have created. Blessed are you, O Lord, who gives food to all.     *A Hebrew Berakoth*

Cʟᴏsɪɴɢ Sᴏɴɢ

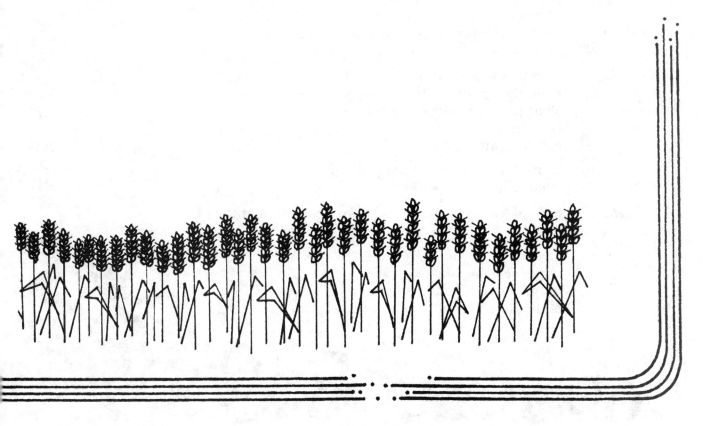

# Reconciled

**Leader**   Father, we come before you in need of your mercy and love. Let us be reconciled to you as we bring peace to our conflicts, charity to those we have offended, compassion to the lonely and those in need. We reach out to you. Guide our way back to your never-ending care. We ask this in the name of our Lord Jesus Christ. Amen.

**Reader**   Isaiah 55:6-13

Silent Reflection

*Shared Response*

**Right**   I give thanks to you, Yahweh,
you were angry with me
but your anger is appeased
and you have given me consolation.

**Left**   See now, he is the God of my salvation
I have trust now and no fear,
for Yahweh is my strength, my song,
he is my salvation.

**Right**   And you will draw water joyfully
from the springs of salvation.
That day, you will say:
Give thanks to Yahweh,
call his name aloud.

**Left**   Proclaim his deeds to the people,
declare his name sublime.

**Right**   Sing of Yahweh, for he has done marvelous things,
let them be made known to the whole world.

**Left**   Cry out for joy and gladness,
you dwellers in Zion,
for great in the midst of you
is the Holy One of Israel.   *from Isaiah 12*

*Reader*   John 8:2-11

SILENT REFLECTION

*Reader*   In the presence of one another, let us ask the Lord's forgiveness by responding, "Father, have mercy on us."
For the times we have worked against one another, we pray . . .
For the times we have been stubborn and let greed overcome us, we pray . . .
For the times we have been quick to judge, criticize, and insult one another, we pray . . .
For the times we have complained about the work of our ministry, we pray . . .
For the times we have neglected the work which is ours, we pray . . .
For the times we have failed to see the importance of all people, we pray . . .
For the times we have forgotten the poor and oppressed, we pray . . .
For the times our lives have not been a reflection of Jesus Christ, we pray . . .

*Leader*   Let us pray together to our Father in the words of our Lord Jesus Christ.

*All*   Our Father . . .

*Leader*   May God our Father bless us and bring us his peace.

*All*   Amen.

*Leader*   May God bring us new life and joy in the days to come.

*All*   Amen.

*Leader*   May almighty God bless us in the name of the Father, and of the Son, and of the Holy Spirit.

*All*   Amen.

# Come Back to Me with All Your Heart

**Leader** "Even now," says the Lord, "come back to me with all your heart. Return to me, the Lord your God." With open arms he awaits our coming. Let us joyfully be reconciled to our God, whose love and mercy are never-ending. He will heal us and refresh us with new life.

**Reader** Hosea 6:1-3

**All** Send your blessing, Lord, as we return to you.

**Reader** Joel 2:12-14

**All** Be with us, Lord, as we come back to you. Heal us. Bring us new life.

**Reader** Jeremiah 4:1-2

**All** Have mercy on us, Lord. Show us your compassion. Be gracious and kind.

**Reader** Sirach 15:11-17

**All** Lord, let us not again be led astray. Let us not choose the ways of the wicked person.

*Psalm Response*

**Right** Have pity on me, O God, in your unfailing love;
in the abundance of your compassion
erase my rebellious deeds.
Wash my guilt away, over and over,
and from my sin make me clean.
How well I know my rebellious acts,
and my sin is ever before me.

**Left** Against you and you alone did I sin,
and I did what you regard as evil.
So, you are just in your sentence
and blameless in your judgment.
In guilt itself was I born,
and in sin my mother conceived me.
Truth pleases you more than cleverness;
you teach wisdom rather than secrets of the occult.

*Right*    Take my sin away
and I will be purer than splashing water;
wash me and I will be whiter than snow.
Let me hear songs of joy and happiness
and the bones you crushed will be overjoyed.
Turn your face away from my sins
and erase all my guilt.

*Left*    Create a clean heart for me, O God,
and put a new and constant spirit in my breast.
Do not banish me from your presence;
do not remove your holy spirit from me.
Restore to me the joy of your deliverance
and uphold me with a generous spirit

*Right*    That I may teach rebels your ways
and sinners to return to you.
Rescue me from the Land of Tears,
O God, my God,
O my Savior, let my tongue shout your generosity.
O Lord, open my lips,
and my mouth shall declare your praise.    *Psalm 51, The Psalms,*
Bonaventure Zerr, O.S.B.

*Leader*    Let us pray for the Father's mercy and love.

SPONTANEOUS PRAYER

*Leader*    Let us together pray the forgiving words of our Lord Jesus Christ.

*All*    Our Father in heaven
may your name be held holy,
your kingdom come,
your will be done
on earth as in heaven.
Give us today our daily bread.
And forgive us our debts,
as we have forgiven those who are in debt to us.
And do not put us to the test,
but save us from the evil one.

*Leader*    May the grace and peace of our Lord Jesus Christ be with us all.

*All*    Now and forever. Amen.

# Compassion and Mercy

*Leader*    Let us pray.

OPENING MEDITATION

*Leader*    Father, we come before you mindful of the times we have been quick to judge one another, of the times our thoughts and feelings for one another have not been those of love. Let compassion and mercy live in our hearts that your love may be the center of our lives. Amen.

*Reader*    Luke 6:35-38

*Psalm Response*

*Right*    I said, "I will watch how I behave,
and not let my tongue lead me into sin;
I will keep a muzzle on my mouth
as long as the wicked man is near me."
I stayed dumb, silent, speechless,
though the sight of him thriving made torment increase.
My heart had been smoldering inside me,
but it flared up at the thought of this
and the words burst out.

*Left*    "Tell me, Yahweh, when my end will be,
how many days are allowed me,
show me how frail I am.
Look, you have given me an inch or two of life,
my life span is nothing to you;
each man that stands on earth is only a puff of wind,

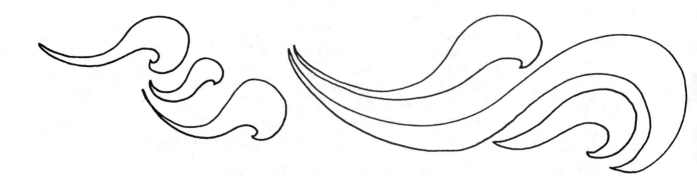

42

every man that walks, only a shadow,
and the wealth he amasses is only a puff of wind--
he does not know who will take it next."

Right    So tell me, Lord, what can I expect?
My hope is in you.
Free me from all my sins,
do not make me the butt of idiots.

Left    Yahweh, hear my prayer,
listen to my cry for help,
do not stay deaf to my crying.
I am your guest, and only for a time,
a nomad like my ancestors.
Look away, let me draw breath,
before I go away and am no more!   *from Psalm 39*

SILENT REFLECTION

Leader    Let us pray for the love and mercy of our Father and one another.

SPONTANEOUS PRAYER

Reader    Ephesians 4:25-32

Leader    Lord, bless and strengthen your people.
May we remain faithful to you and always rejoice in your mercy.
We ask this in the name of the Lord Jesus.

All    Amen.

# The Gift We Offer

**Leader**   Lord, you have called us each by name and drawn us together in your love. Be with us now as we give our lives to you and your people.

**Reader**   Romans 12:4-12

REFLECTION

**All**   We offer you, Lord, a poor man's gift. We offer you a poor man's life. We're poor and hungry; we're naked and weak; we break easily, Lord, so handle us gently.

The goods that we offer are gifts from you: our lives with all their freedom, our distracted minds, our often weak wills, and failing memories. These are a poor man's gift to you.

And since they come from you, Lord, please see your way clear to accepting them. We've had our problems using them well, but we know your love can transform them into a gift pleasing to you.

And as for us, Lord, hear our servant's simple prayer: When we are weak, be our strength; when we doubt, be our faith; when we're discouraged, be our hope; and when we're lost, come and find us. When we're hungry, be our food; and when we're thirsty, be our drink; when we're in darkness, be our light; and when we're sad, be our comfort and joy.

Let us feel your touch in all we say and do. Let us grow and blossom in your love. Grant us this, Lord, and there's nothing more we want until we see you face to face. Take all we have and are, give us your love and your grace, with all these we are full, yes, we're full.   *Suspice, God of Seasons*, Michael E. Moynahan, S.J.

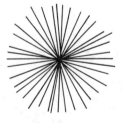

*Reader*    Matthew 5:13-16

REFLECTION

*Leader*    Let us pray.

SPONTANEOUS PRAYER

*Leader*    For all that has been—Thanks.
To all that shall be—Yes.
To say Yes to life is at one and the same time to say Yes to
    oneself.
Yes—even to that element in one which is most unwilling to let
    itself be transformed from a temptation into a strength.
To be free, to be able to stand up and leave everything behind—
    without looking back.
To say Yes.    *Dag Hammarskjold*

*All*    Glory be to the Father, and to the Son, and to the Holy Spirit. As it
was in the beginning, is now, and ever shall be, world without end.
Amen.

# In Your Name

OPENING MEDITATION

*Leader*  May the grace of our Lord Jesus Christ be with you all.

*All*  And also with you.

*Leader*  We are a gifted people, Lord, and you have done great deeds for us. And all you ask is that we reach out to you in your people. Let us touch those in need as we act in your name.

*Reader*  Celebration must be combined with service.
The relationship between man and God is a two-way street.
Our great God gives;
   we must respond to His gracious gifts.
Our response is the offering of our lives,
   the placing of ourselves at His disposal,
   for the accomplishment of His purposes
   in the world about us.
We are, once we acknowledge God's love
   and accept His salvation,
   under new management.
This is what worship is all about.
It is not confined
   to loud singing or verbal exclamations.
It is turning our hearts, minds, and bodies
   over to God's ownership,
   and dedicating our abilities and gifts to His service.
We have all received such gifts for this very purpose.
They are not given to us to enhance our beauty
   or assure our worldly security,
   or even to make us more desirable or respected
   among the people with whom we live and labor.
They are committed to us
   in order to be committed back to God
   in and through and by way of service
   to our fellowmen for God's sake.
This is precisely the way in which our God meets
   the needs of our neighbor—through us
   and through these gifts entrusted to us.
Not all of us have these gifts entrusted to us.
   to administer or preach
   or teach or finance important projects.
But we all have specific abilities—
   love, energy, persistence, patience,
   sincerity, concern, creativity.

We are to exercise these things upon one another
  and on behalf of one another.
We are to care for each other
  even as much as we care for ourselves.
We are to allow our God to reach and touch others,
  even our very enemies,
  with His care and concern for them through us.   *Romans 12,*
                                     *Epistles/Now,* Leslie F. Brandt

SILENT REFLECTION

*Reader*   Matthew 25:31-46

SILENT REFLECTION

*Reader 1*   A Strange Kind of King
Lord, the picture we have of you today in your gospel, in which we
see you as a king, coming in glory, escorted by angels, seated on a
throne and having authority over all nations of this world, that
picture is a future vision as you will come at the end of time.
But, Lord, what about us, your followers today? We wait for that
day when your kingdom will be everywhere here on earth; when
all people will live in love, unity and peace with one another.
But what about the meantime—today? Tomorrow?

Your gospel today has a flashback, and it tells us what you were,
and where you were before those final days, that end of time.
In that flashback we see you described as a very strange king. Instead of having plenty of the finest food and drink, you say you are
hungry and thirsty, desperately hungry, and you just didn't miss
breakfast or diet for a few days.

We may not have realized it, but not long ago there were pictures
on TV of people, children, who looked like living skeletons.
And so I wonder what you are today. Are you starving with the
thousands of men, women and children in the drought and worn-
torn places on this earth? We hear and read about refugee camps
in Lebanon, Thailand or El Salvador. We hear and read about
Cubans and Haitians coming to our country, looking for a home, a
job. Many are adrift, homeless. Some were lost at sea not too long
ago and were washed up, dead, on the beach somewhere near
Miami; one was even holding a Bible in his hand. Were you among
them?
Often in our city we see poor people, who have wornout shoes, old
and tattered clothes, who wander the streets and seem to have no

47

home or friend. If we can't find you among them would we check the hospitals?

O yes, your gospel does say that you were sick. Maybe you couldn't afford the expense of staying in the hospital. Is there anyone to take care of you?

And finally, of all places, we're supposed to find you in prison. That sounds unbelievable. "I was in prison." Kings don't go to prison, they put others there.

Is it true you've seen more than one prison from the inside? Those forty years in the death camps with your own people, the Jews? With political prisoners today? Are you among the innocent, or even the guilty, as you once were between two thieves on a hill called Calvary?

What a strange kind of king. One who is hungry, thirsty, naked, homeless, lonely, sick, in prison . . .

Reader 2      (The Lord speaks to the Christian.)
Yes, my friend, you see I am a different kind of king. My palace could be in your city, or your neighborhood. I'm waiting for you to help me out.

You see, wherever there is a needy person on this earth, I am not only *with* that person, but I am that person waiting to be helped. But you don't have to help me unless you freely choose to help. The choice is always yours. But, please, please make it carefully, because one day I will stand before you and ask for an answer. I'm quite sure you'll want to be with those to whom I'll say,

Come, inherit the kingdom prepared for you from the beginning of the world--because whatsoever you did to the least of my brothers and sisters in this world, that you did to me, your king.

Rev. Don Schmidt

SILENT REFLECTION

Leader      Let us pray.

SPONTANEOUS PRAYER

Leader      As a people called to respond to the Father, let us do so with the words Jesus taught us.

All      Our Father . . .

# A Light to All Nations

*Leader*    Father, we come before you today, in the presence of this community, to reaffirm our commitment to your work. We are Jesus Christ in the world today. We are a light to all nations. With the guidance and support of your Spirit we bring your word to all people. Let us not forget you are always with us. Let our lights burn forever with your love. We ask this through Jesus Christ, the light of lights, our Lord and brother. Amen.

LIGHTING OF CANDLES

Once your candle is lit, spread that light to another with the words "receive the light of Christ." Let the candles burn throughout the readings.

*Reader*    Persons are gifts . . . at least Jesus thought so: "Father, I want those you have given me to be where I am . . ." I agree with Jesus . . . and I also want those whom the Father has given me to be where I am.

Persons are gifts which the Father sends me wrapped. Some are wrapped very beautifully; they are very attractive when I first see them. Some come in very ordinary wrapping paper. Others have been mishandled in the mail. Once in a while there is a "Special Delivery." Some persons are gifts which come very loosely wrapped; others very tightly.

But the wrapping is not the gift! It is so easy to make this mistake. It's amusing when babies do it. Sometimes the gift is very easy to open up. Sometimes I need others to help. Is it because they are afraid? Does it hurt? Maybe they have been opened up before and thrown away! Could it be that the gift is not for me?

I am a person. Therefore, I am a gift, too. A gift for myself first of all. The Father gave myself to me. Have I ever really looked inside the wrappings? Afraid to? Perhaps I've never accepted the gift that I am. Could it be that there is something else inside the wrappings than what I think there is? Maybe I've never seen the wonderful gift that I am? Could the Father's gifts be anything but beautiful?

I love those gifts which those who love me give me; why not this gift from the Father? And I am a gift to other persons. Am I willing to be given by . . . the Father to others . . . a person for others? Do others have to be content with the wrappings . . . never permitted to enjoy the gift? Every meeting of persons is an exchange of gifts.

*Author unknown*

50

SILENT REFLECTION

Reader     Matthew 5:14-16

          OUR STATEMENT OF COMMITMENT (All respond "We do" after each statement.)

Leader     Do you believe in God, the Father, maker of heaven and earth, the source of our being?
Do you believe in Jesus Christ, his Son, the light of life, the light of all lights?
Do you believe in the Spirit whose presence is felt in our enthusiasm and in our work?
Do you commit yourself to bringing the word of God to his children on earth?
Do you promise to care for others in the way of Jesus Christ?
Do you promise to witness the gospel even in the face of harrassment, frustration, and apathy?
Do you promise to remain open to the Spirit?
Do you commit yourself to the support of our Christian community?
As a seal of our commitment, then let us join in saying the prayer of our community, the prayer Jesus taught us.

All     Our Father . . .

Leader     God has called us out of darkness into his wonderful light. May we experience his kindness and blessings, and be strong in faith, in hope, and in love.

All     Amen.

51

# The Breath of God in Us

*Leader*    Father, as we gather today, we ask for your blessing. We come together to celebrate our call to bring your love to all people. In doing your work, though, we encounter obstacles and setbacks. It is at times such as these we need your support and that of your community. Let us be reassured of that support, Lord, that we may continue with enthusiasm and confidence, for in bringing your work to the world we find the joy of your kingdom. We ask this through Jesus Christ our Lord and brother. Amen.

*Reader*    Today let us breathe deeply the breath of God in us, for through us God inhales the fantasies of children, the experiences of yesterday and the hopes of tomorrow.

Let us rejoice over this breath in us lest God wonder whether his world has grown too old and his people too despairing to celebrate.

Let us spin him our dream.

That someday soon all people will celebrate life everyday.

That someday soon all people will know they are beautiful in black and red and white.

That someday we will glimpse the face of God in our students, patients, co-workers and clients.

Someday soon we will airlift food to starving people.

Someday soon we will grow wheat in deserts and flowers in garbage cans.

Soon we will turn our tired old cathedrals into cafeterias for the poor . . . and for the rich.

Soon we will sink our teeth and our talents into the politics of peace and justice.

Someday soon we will light our homes with the sun and lighten our hearts with love.

Someday soon "we will live more simply, so that others may simply live."

Someday soon we will turn our guns into large tubes of finger paint.

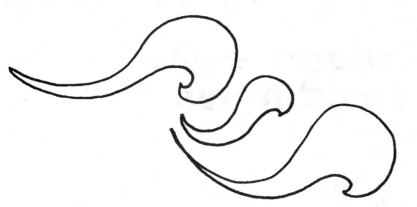

Someday we will use the eyes of our friends in place of mirrors.
Someday we will become as free as that man called Jesus Christ
    and in our freedom we will liberate others.
Soon, yes, very soon, we will slow down and wait and we will
    hear Your voice in us, dear Lord.
Yes, someday soon, we will dance in the August evening and
    live in risk before the sun sets.
Someday we will live like that—or we will not live at all.
These are our dreams, Lord, our dreams are our gifts.
Today is your gift. Someday begins today.    *Author Unknown*

SILENT REFLECTION

*Reader*    1 Corinthians 12:4-11

*Leader*    Father, your work has become our work. We are Jesus Christ in the world today. But our needs are many. We bring our prayers before you, Lord, that you may be with us, guide us, and give us strength. As we present our needs, let us respond, "Lord, be with us."

SPONTANEOUS PRAYER

*Leader*    Knowing the Father is with us, let us pray to him in the way Jesus taught us.

*All*    Our Father . . .

*Leader*    Lord, we pray for your people who believe in you.
May we all enjoy the gift of your love,
Share it with others,
And spread it everywhere.
We ask this in the name of Jesus the Lord.

*All*    Amen.

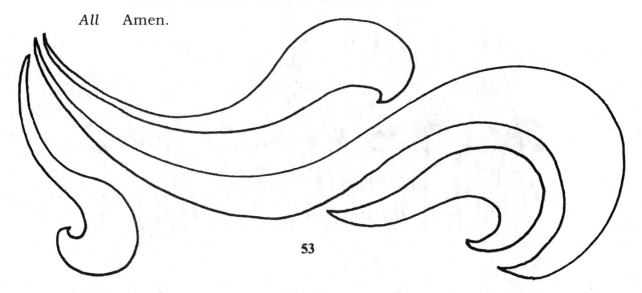

# Announce the Good News

OPENING MEDITATION

Leader    The Lord be with you.

All    And also with you.

Leader    Father, you have called us to bring your word to all people. You have asked us to carry on the mission of Jesus Christ. But there are times we lack strength and conviction. Many refuse to listen. Send your Spirit among us that we may be a strong people in bringing your word. Open the ears, eyes, and hearts of those we will speak to so that they too may rejoice in you. We ask this in the name of our Lord, Jesus Christ. Amen.

Reader    Romans 10:14-21

REFLECTION

*Shared Response*

Right    A voice cries, "Prepare in the wilderness a way for Yahweh.
Make a straight highway for our God across the desert.
Let every valley be filled in, every mountain and hill be laid low,
let every cliff become a plain,
and the ridges a valley.

Left    Then the glory of Yahweh shall be revealed
and all mankind shall see it;
for the mouth of Yahweh has spoken."
A voice commands: "Cry!"
and I answered, "What shall I cry?"
"All flesh is grass
and its beauty like the wild flower's.

Right    The grass withers, the flower fades
when the breath of Yahweh blows on them.

The grass withers,the flower fades,
but the word of our God remains for ever."

*Left*     Go up on a high mountain,
joyful messenger to Zion. Shout with a loud voice,
joyful messenger to Jerusalem.
Shout without fear,
say to the towns of Judah,
"Here is your God."    *from Isaiah 40*

*Reader*    Matthew 13:13-16

Reflection

*Leader*    Let us pray. Knowing that the Father hears us and answers our
needs, let us bring to him our prayers of petition.

Spontaneous Prayer

*Leader*    In praise and thanksgiving, let us pray together the words Jesus
gave us.

*All*    Our Father in heaven,
may your name be held holy,
your kingdom come,
your will be done
on earth as in heaven.
Give us today our daily bread.
And forgive those who are in debt to us.
And do not put us to the test,
but save us from the evil one.

*Reader*    Romans 16:25-27

des, but the word remains forever.

# Beginning

| | |
|---|---|
| *Leader* | Father, bless this gathering with your presence |
| *All* | That our work may be the work of the Lord. |

*Leader*  Let us pray. Father, all that lies ahead of us is yet unseen. May we come to know one another and the ministry we have been called to. Let us not forget you have asked us to be the servants and not the masters. We are here to work for the good of all our community. Be with us as our counselor and our support as we begin our journey. We ask this through Jesus Christ, our Lord and brother. Amen.

*Reader*  Our relationship to our fellow human beings with the body of
    Christ is of paramount importance.
Our roles as the ministers of Christ,
    our assignments as His beloved servants
    may vary greatly.
Some of us are leaders who have been granted a position of
    authority over others.
We ought to be aware that our social and educational status,
    regardless of what it means to our peers, does not impress our
    Lord; every one of His children is equally important to Him.
And we need to be reminded, from time to time, that with
    leadership comes responsibility, the responsibility to treat
    those who work under us as equals before God, and to love
    them as such, our brothers and sisters in Christ.
We are, every one of us, the minister of God.
There are those who serve God even in the process of serving us.
They are those who make it possible for us to fulfill our responsi-
    bilities in our arena of service.
We need each other, parent and child, employer and employee,
    master and servant.
We must, together, submit to the Master of masters, the Lord of
    lords, our Redeemer and King, our Father and our God.
Together we seek to fulfill his objectives and advance His
    kingdom upon our world.
We do so as members of the same family,
    the family of God and Christ.   *Philemon, Epistles/Now,*
                                Leslie F. Brandt

*Psalm Response*

**Left**  May God show kindness and bless us,
and make his face smile on us!

**Right**  For then the earth will acknowledge your ways
and all the nations will know of your power to save.
Let the nations praise you, O God,
let all the nations praise you!

**Left**  Let the nations shout and sing for joy,
since you dispense true justice to the world;
you dispense strict justice to the peoples,
on earth you rule the nations.
Let the nations praise you, God,
Let all the nations praise you!

**Right**  The soil has given its harvest,
God, our God, has blessed us.
May God bless us, and let him be feared
to the very ends of the earth.     *Psalm 67*

**Reader**  John 13:1-17

SILENT REFLECTION

**Leader**  Let us pray for the guidance and support of our Father.

SPONTANEOUS PRAYER

**Leader**  In the words of Jesus Christ, let us together pray . . .

**All**  Our Father . . .

**Leader**  Lord, bless and strengthen your people.

**All**  Let your face shine upon us and bring us peace.

# Sing Glory to God

*Leader*    Sing joyfully to God, all you on earth.
Sing praise to the glory of his name.

OPENING SONG

*Reader*    1 Chronicles 29:10-13

REFLECTION

*Reader*    All of you who are upright, sing for joy to Yahweh!
Give praise to the Glorious One,
all of you who are upright.
Praise Yahweh with a harp;
on a lute of ten strings play to him!
Sing him a new song!
Make beautiful music with gladness!
The word of Yahweh is true;
the works of his hands are worthy of trust.
He loves what is just and what is right.
The earth is full of Yahweh's unfailing love.
At the word of Yahweh the heavens were made;
a breath of his created all the lights that are in them.
He confined the waters of the seas in a vessel;
he put the primeval abyss in his storehouses.
Give reverence to Yahweh, all the earth;
all the peoples of the world, stand in awe of him.
For he is the one who spoke,
and everything came to be;
he is the one who gave the command,
and there stood everything.
Yahweh breaks up the plan of the nations;
he frustrates the schemes of the peoples.
The plan of Yahweh will stand forever;
the designs of his heart will last age after age.
Happy the people he has chosen to be his own!
Our hearts rejoice in him;
we trust in his holy name.
Let your unfailing love come upon us, Yahweh,
just as we have put our hope in you.   *Psalm 33, The Psalms,*
Bonaventure Zerr, O.S.B.

REFLECTION

*Reader*    Luke 1:46-55

REFLECTION

*Leader*    In the spirit of praise and thanksgiving, let us pray to our God from whom all good things come.

SPONTANEOUS PRAYER

*Leader*    May the peace and glory of God which is beyond all understanding keep our hearts and minds in the knowledge and love of God and his Son our Lord Jesus Christ.

*All*    Amen.

# In Thanksgiving

OPENING SONG

**Leader**    Father, you have blessed us with your love and compassion. You have chosen us to be a people of your own. Hear our prayers of thanksgiving as we give glory and praise to you.

**Reader**    Deuteronomy 4:32-40

*Psalm Response*

**Right**    Give thanks to Yahweh, call his name aloud,
proclaim his deeds to the peoples!
Sing to him, play to him,
tell over all his marvels!
Glory in his holy name,
let the hearts that seek Yahweh rejoice!

**Left**    Seek Yahweh and his strength,
seek his face untiringly;
remember the marvels he has done,
his wonder, the judgments from his mouth.

**Right**    He is Yahweh our God,
his authority is over all the earth.
Remember his covenant for ever,
his word of command for a thousand generations,
the pact he made with Abraham,
his oath to Isaac.
He established it as a statute for Jacob,
an everlasting covenant for Israel.
"I give you a land," he said,
"Canaan, your allotted heritage.

**Left**    "There where you were easily counted,
few in number, strangers to the country."
They went from nation to nation,
from one kingdom to another people:
he let no man oppress them,
he punished kings on their behalf.
"Do not touch my anointed ones," he said,
"do not harm my prophets!"   *from Psalm 105*

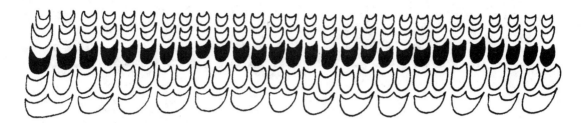

Reader  Colossians 3:12-17

*Psalm Response*

All  I thank you, Yahweh, with all my heart,
because you have heard what I said.
In the presence of the angels I play for you,
and bow down toward your holy Temple.
I give thanks to your name for your love and faithfulness;
your promise is even greater than your fame.
The day I called for help, you heard me
and you increased my strength.
Yahweh, all kings on earth give thanks to you,
for they have heard your promises;
they celebrate Yahweh's actions,
"Great is the glory of Yahweh!"
From far above, Yahweh sees the humble,
from far away he marks down the arrogant.  *from Psalm 138*

Leader  In praise and thanksgiving, let us pray.

SPONTANEOUS PRAYER

All  I give thanks to Yahweh with all my heart
where the virtuous meet and the people assemble.
The works of Yahweh are sublime,
those who delight in them are right to fix their eyes on them.
Every work that he does is full of glory and majesty,
and his righteousness can never change.
He allows us to commemorate his marvels.
Yahweh is merciful and tenderhearted.  *from Psalm 111*

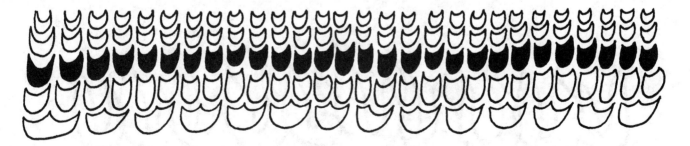

# The Spirit Among Us

OPENING MEDITATION

**Leader**  Here is my servant whom I uphold, my chosen one in whom my soul delights. I have endowed him with my spirit that he may bring true justice to the nations.     *Isaiah 42:1*

**All**  The spirit of the Lord Yahweh has been given to me, for Yahweh anointed me. He has sent me to bring good news to the poor, to bind up hearts that are broken; to proclaim liberty to captives, freedom to those in prison; to proclaim a year of favor from Yahweh, a day of vengeance for our God, to comfort all those who mourn and to give them for ashes a garland; for mourning robe the oil of gladness, for despondency, praise.     *Isaiah 61:1-3*

**Leader**  Thus says God, Yahweh, he who created the heavens and spread them out, who gave shape to the earth and what comes from it, who gave breath to its people and life to the creatures that move in it: I, Yahweh, have called you to serve the cause of right; I have taken you by the hand and formed you; I have appointed you as a covenant of the people and light of the nations.     *Isaiah 42:5-6*

**Reader**  John 16:4-16

REFLECTION

**Reader**  Acts 2:1-4

REFLECTION

*Reader*    God is here, near us, unforeseeable and loving. I am a man of hope, not for human reasons nor from any natural optimism, but because I believe the Holy Spirit is at work in the Church and in the world, even where His name remains unheard. I am an optimist because I believe the Holy Spirit is the Spirit of creation. To those who welcome him he gives each day fresh liberty and renewed joy and trust. The long history of the Church is filled with the wonders of the Holy Spirit. Think only of the prophets and saints who, in times of darkness, have discovered a spring of grace and shed beams of light on our path. John XXIII came as a surprise, and the Council, too. They were the last things we expected. Who would dare to say that the love and imagination of God were exhausted? To hope is a duty, not a luxury. To hope is not to dream, but to turn dreams into reality. Happy are those who dream dreams and are ready to pay the price to make them come true.

*Leo Cardinal Suenens*

*All*    Father of light, from whom every good gift comes, send your Spirit into our lives. With the power of the mighty wind and by the flame of your wisdom, open the horizons of our minds. Loosen our tongues to sing your praise beyond the power of speech, for without your Spirit we could never raise our voice in words of peace and announce the truth that Jesus is Lord, who lives and reigns with you and the Holy Spirit, one God, forever and ever. Amen.

*Prayer on the Feast of Pentecost*

CLOSING SONG

# *Prayer for Unity*

OPENING MEDITATION

*Leader*   The Lord be with you.

*All*   And also with you.

*Leader*   Let us pray. Father, we pray today that your Church may once again be united as a people called to be one in your Spirit. Let us put that which divides behind us as we learn to work for the good of all people. May peace and understanding come to our lives so that we may realize our oneness in you. We ask this through Jesus Christ, our Lord and brother. Amen.

*Reader*   John 17:20-26

SILENT REFLECTION

*Reader*   Ephesians 4:1-4

REFLECTION

*Leader*   Let us pray to the Lord our God.

SPONTANEOUS PRAYER

*Leader*   Together let us pray the prayer common to all Christians.

*All*   Our Father who are in heaven, hallowed be your name: your kingdom come; your will be done on earth as it is in heaven. Give us this day our daily bread; and forgive us our trespasses as we forgive those who trespass against us; and lead us not into temptation, but deliver us from evil. For yours is the kingdom, the power and the glory, now and forever. Amen.

# Dream Dreams

**Leader**   The Lord be with you.

**All**   And also with you.

**Leader**   He gathers us into his kingdom.

**All**   That we may know the love and glory of the Father.

**Leader**   Let us pray. O Lord, let our dreams soar. Let all our inhibitions and fears disappear as we strive to make our hopes come into being. Give us the strength, courage and insight we will need as we work to bring our vision to reality. Let your Spirit guide us in our imaginations and our fantasies so that worries and anxieties will not overcome us, for it is only through dreams that the beauty and wonder of your kingdom will be made known to all mankind. Be with us, Lord, as our minds wander, as we dream *your* dreams.

**Reader**   Dreams come and go in our lives.
Far more die
than come to reality.
What is it in us that allows us to let go of visions
that could create new and beautiful worlds?
Why do we so easily give in to barriers?
Why do we let ourselves conform and be satisfied
with what is?
Reaching out to a dream can be risky.
It can involve hardships
that our imaginations never knew.
Our comfortableness can so easily be disturbed.
But, what beauty can be experienced as we accept
the challenge of a dream!
What a precious feeling to be supported,
to have others say you can do it,
we can do it together.
Nothing is beyond our reach
if we reach out together,

*Dream dreams Dream dreams Dream dreams Drea*

66

if we reach out with all the confidence we have,
if we are willing to persevere even in difficult times
and if we rejoice with every small step forward,
if we dream beautiful dreams that will transform
   our lives, our world.
Nothing is impossible
  if we put aside our careful ways,
  if we build our dreams with faith--
    faith in ourselves,
    faith in our sisters and brothers,
    and above all,
    faith in our Lord God
      with whom all things are possible.

SILENT REFLECTION

*Reader*   Matthew 7:7-11 and 18:19-20

SILENT REFLECTION

*Leader*   Let us pray.

SPONTANEOUS PRAYER

*All*   Lord, the more we dream the farther our hopes will take us. Let us be carried on the wings of our dreams with a confidence yet unknown. May we accept our challenges with unfounded enthusiasm and naive expectations, for nothing is impossible in your midst. Let us be blind to obstacles and limitations as we build your glorious kingdom. May our romanticism be seen and received. We ask this through Jesus Christ, our Lord and brother, the ultimate dreamer. Amen.

*reams Dream dreams Dream dreams Dream dreams*

# Live Simply

**Leader**   Let us pray. Lord Jesus, teach us your simple ways. Let us learn to live more simply. Let us become like children once again, excited about the new and simple and always certain there is a Father who will love and care for us. Together, we ask this in your name. Amen.

**Reader**   If I had my life to live over again, I'd make more mistakes next time. I would relax. I would limber up. I would be sillier than I have been this time around. I know of very few things I would take seriously. I would take more trips. I would climb more mountains, swim more rivers, watch more sunsets, run more beaches, bathe in more moonlight and wink back at more stars.

I would do more walking and looking and sitting. If I had it to do over again, I would go places, do things and travel lighter than I have. If I had my life to live over, I would start going barefoot earlier in the spring and stay that way later in the fall.

I would have more actual troubles and fewer imaginary ones. I would enjoy moments, one after another, instead of living so many years ahead each day.

But most of all, I would have more time for people and more time for God.   *Yoga Philosophy*

REFLECTION

**Reader**   Why, Jesus, did you love children so? Why did you say we had to become childlike to understand you? Are you trying to teach us to approach you in a simply way, without affectation, without "big" ideas? Children are attracted to people who are kind and generous and loving toward them. How easily they recognize insincerity and sham!

But we are to imitate both you and children. Simple in approaching you, loving and generous and kind toward others--that must be our double program.

It is so much easier, Jesus, to defend rights and carry placards than to be kind and loving and simple and childlike. Teach us to be your kind of hero; and thanks for cutting us down to size.     *Walking on the Wings of the Wind*, Archbishop Rembert G. Weakland, O.S.B.

REFLECTION

*Reader*     Mark 10:13-16

REFLECTION

*Leader*     Let us pray.

SPONTANEOUS PRAYER

*Leader*     May the Lord order our days in his peace,
hear our every prayer
and lead us to everlasting life and joy.

*All*     Amen.

# Prayer in Times of Decision Making

**Leader**   The grace and peace of the Lord Jesus Christ be with you all.

**All**   And also with you.

**Leader**   Let us pray. Lord, as we begin today, we ask for the wisdom, understanding and guidance of your Spirit. Open our minds and hearts that we may see clearly. Let your will be made known to us that we may make our choices in accordance with your ways. Let us be truly Christian in this gathering. We ask this through Jesus Christ our Lord and counselor. Amen

**Reader**   Romans 12:1-2

*Psalm Response*

**All**   To you, Yahweh, I lift up my soul, O my God.
I rely on you, do not let me be shamed,
do not let my enemies gloat over me!
No, those who hope in you are never shamed,
shame awaits disappointed traitors.
Yahweh, make your ways known to me,
teach me your paths.
Set me in the way of your truth, and teach me,
for you are the God who saves me.
All day long I hope in you
because of your goodness, Yahweh.   *from Psalm 25*

REFLECTION

**Leader**   Lord, hear our prayers as we ask for your guidance and support.

SPONTANEOUS PRAYER

**Leader**   Let us pray.

**All**   Our Father . . .

**Leader**   Lord, send your Spirit among us.

**All**   That we may grow in wisdom and understanding.

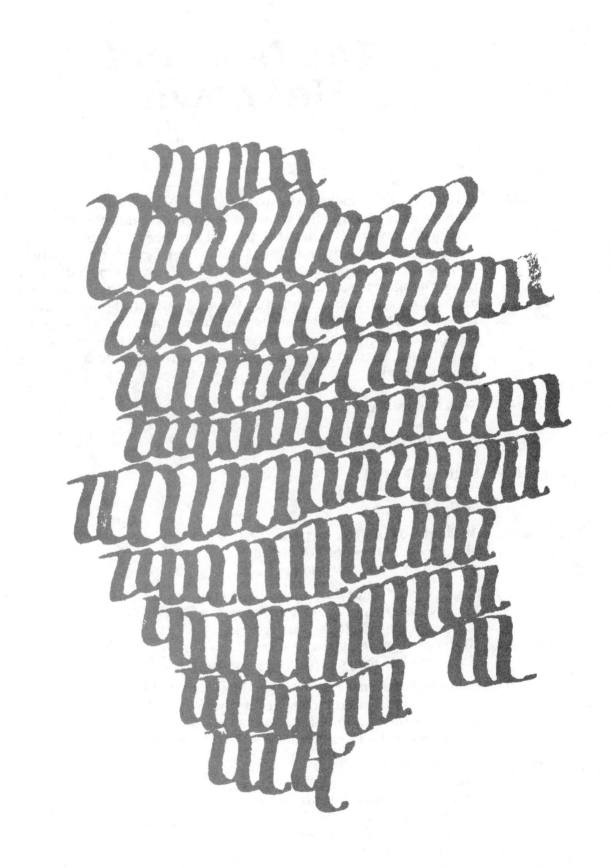

# The New and Unknown

OPENING MEDITATION

*Leader*  Father, we have looked at ourselves and have realized that it is time for us to change. But we want to hold on to our old ways, our comfortable ways. It's not that the old has been bad, but that we are living in a new day; that which has been brought us to where we now are. We need to look at ourselves again and continue on, to make changes, to step into the new and unknown to make our lives all the more rich and meaningful. We are hesitant, though, Lord. It is easier to stay where we are for we know that what is was good. We wonder whether our new ways will be the same or if we will fail. Be with us, Lord, as we continue on, as we change and as we hopefully grow.

*Reader*  Ecclesiastes 3:1-8

SILENT REFLECTION

*Reader*  Matthew 6:26-34

*Psalm Response*

*Left*  Acclaim God, all the earth,
play music to the glory of his name,
glorify him with your praises.

*Right*  Say to God, "What dread you inspire!"
Your achievements are the measure of your power.
Your enemies cringe in your presence;
all the earth bows down to you,
playing music for you, playing in honor of your name.

*Left*  Come and see what marvels God has done,
so much to be feared for his deeds among mankind:
he turned the sea into dry land,
they crossed the river on foot!

*Right*  So let us rejoice in him,
who rules for ever by his power:
his eyes keep watch on the nations,
let no rebel raise his head!
You nations, bless our God
and make his praise resound.

*Left*    Who brings our soul to life
and keeps our feet from faltering.
You tested us, God,
you refined us like silver.

*Right*    You let us fall into the net
you laid heavy burdens on our backs,
you let people drive over our heads;
but now the ordeal by fire and water is over,
and you allow us once more to draw breath.

*All*    Come and listen, all you who fear God,
while I tell you what he has done for me:
when I uttered my cry to him
and high praise was on my tongue,
had I been guilty in my heart,
the Lord would never have heard me.
But God not only heard me,
he listened to my prayer.
Blessed be God,
who neither ignored my prayer
nor deprived me of his love.   *from Psalm 66*

*Leader*    Let us pray . . .

SPONTANEOUS PRAYER

*Leader*    Father, hear our prayers and send your Spirit to guide us as we chance the unknown ahead. Listen to us once again as we pray that your will, and not ours, be done.

*All*    Our Father in heaven,
may your name be held holy,
your kingdom come,
your will be done
on earth as in heaven.
Give us this day our daily bread.
And forgive us our debts,
as we have forgiven those who are in debt to us.
And do not put us to the test,
but save us from the evil one.
Amen.

# Prayer in Times of Frustration and Doubt

*Leader*   We gather in the presence of our Father. May he hear our prayers and strengthen his people.

*All*   Lord, bring us hope and understanding that our vision may be clear and our minds be open.

*Leader*   God our Father, we ask you today to bring us hope in the midst of discouragement, perseverance when we become frustrated and reminders of your love when we encounter hard times. Let those of this community be the support of one another. Send your wisdom and guidance. Be at our sides now and always. We ask this in the name of our Lord Jesus Christ. Amen.

*Reader*   2 Corinthians 4

SILENT REFLECTION

*Leader*   Let us pray. Father, hear the prayers of your people and grant us peace that we may continue your work in hope and confidence.

SPONTANEOUS PRAYER

*Leader*   Together let us pray the words Jesus gave us.

*All*   Our Father . . .

*Reader*   Philippians 4:4-9

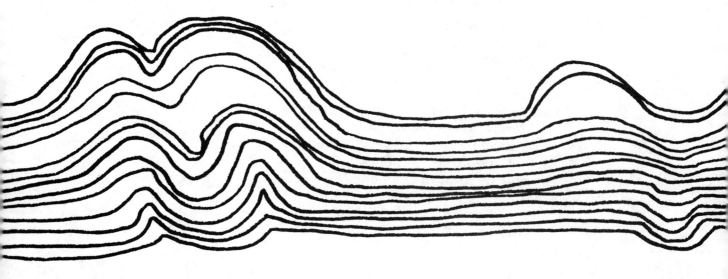

# Prayer in Times of Illness

OPENING MEDITATION

Leader    Father, just as your Son, Jesus, cured the blind, the lame, the sick and the dying, you continue to bring us your healing Spirit. Take care of us and all your people as we face the threat of sickness and pain. Help us to respond to the love and care you show in times of illness and of health. We ask this through Jesus Christ. Amen.

Reader    James 5:13-16

SILENT REFLECTION

Reader    John 9:1-7

SILENT REFLECTION

Leader    Let us pray.

SPONTANEOUS PRAYER

**All**    Lord, suffering disturbs me. I don't understand why you allow it. Why, Lord? I don't understand. Why this suffering in the world that shocks, isolates, revolts, shatters? Why this hideous suffering that strikes blindly without seeming cause, falling unjustly on the good and sparing the evil; which seems to withdraw, conquered by science, but comes back in another form, more powerful and more subtle? I don't understand. Suffering is odious and frightens me. Why these people, Lord, and not others? Why these, and not me?

**Reader**    Son, it is not I, your God who has willed suffering; it is men. They have brought it into the world in bringing sin, because sin is disorder, and disorder hurts. There is for every sin, somewhere in the world and in time, a corresponding suffering. And the more sins there are, the more suffering.

But I came, and I took all your sufferings upon me, as I took all your sins, I took them and suffered them before you. I transformed them, I made them a treasure. They are still an evil, but an evil with a purpose, for through your sufferings, I accomplished Redemption.    *The Hospital, Prayers,* Michel Quoist

**Leader**    Father, bring us your blessing always. Keep us and our families in good health. May those who are suffering know your love and compassion through us. Help us endure any pain we may experience. We ask this through Jesus Christ our Lord and healer. Amen.

# I Go to Prepare a Place for You

OPENING MEDITATION

**Leader**   Lord, we ask you today to grant eternal life onto _____. In life he/she came to know of your love. May he/she now know life in all its fullness, in all its glory. We pray, too, for the family and friends of _____ as they experience the loss of their loved one. May they be consoled in their sorrow. Along with them, we wish _____ the peace of the Lord God forever and ever. Amen.

**Reader**   2 Corinthians 5:1, 6-10

*Psalm Response*

**Reader**   To you, Yahweh, I lift up my soul.

**All**   To you, Yahweh, I lift up my soul.

**Reader**   Remember your kindness, Yahweh,
your love, that you promised long ago.
Do not remember the sins of my youth;
but rather, with your love remember me.

**All**   To you, Yahweh, I lift up my soul.

**Reader**   Relieve the distress of my heart,
free me from my sufferings.
See my misery and pain,
forgive all my sins!

*All*    To you, Yahweh, I lift up my soul.

*Reader*    Watch over my soul, rescue me;
let me not be shamed: I take shelter in you.
Let innocence and integrity be my protection,
since my hope is in you, Yahweh.

*All*    To you, Yahweh, I lift up my soul.     *from Psalm 25*

*Reader*    John 14:1-6

Silent Reflection

*Leader*    Let us pray.

Spontaneous Prayer

*Leader*    In his great love, the God of all consolation gave all the gift of life.
May he bless you with faith in the resurrection of his Son and with
the hope of rising to new life.

*All*    Amen.

*Leader*    To us who are alive may he grant forgiveness and to all who have
died a place of light and peace.

*All*    Amen.

# Celebration! Prayer When Work is Completed

OPENING SONG

Leader    Lord, as we gather today we celebrate the work we have completed. We rejoice and are grateful for the good that has been accomplished in your name. There were times when we were doubtful and frustrated because of the obstacles we encountered. But, with the wisdom and guidance of your Spirit, we found joy in our work . . . your work. And so, Father, we celebrate and give you thanks.

Reader    1 John 1:1-5

*Psalm Response*

All    Sing Yahweh a new song,
let the congregation of the faithful sing his praise!
Let Israel rejoice in his maker,
and Zion's children exult in their King;
let them dance in praise of his name,
playing to him on strings and drums!
For Yahweh has been kind to his people,
conferring victory on us who are weak;
the faithful exult in triumph.
Thus gloriously are the faithful rewarded!
Alleluia.    *from Psalm 149*

Reader    1 John 2:24-27

SILENT REFLECTION

Leader    In praise and thanksgiving, let us pray to our Father.

SPONTANEOUS PRAYER

Leader    Together let us pray the words Jesus taught us to say.

All    Our Father . . .

Leader    The peace and joy of the Lord Jesus Christ be with you all.

All    And also with you.

Leader    Let us continue our work with even greater enthusiasm and confidence as we strive to build the kingdom.

All    Amen.

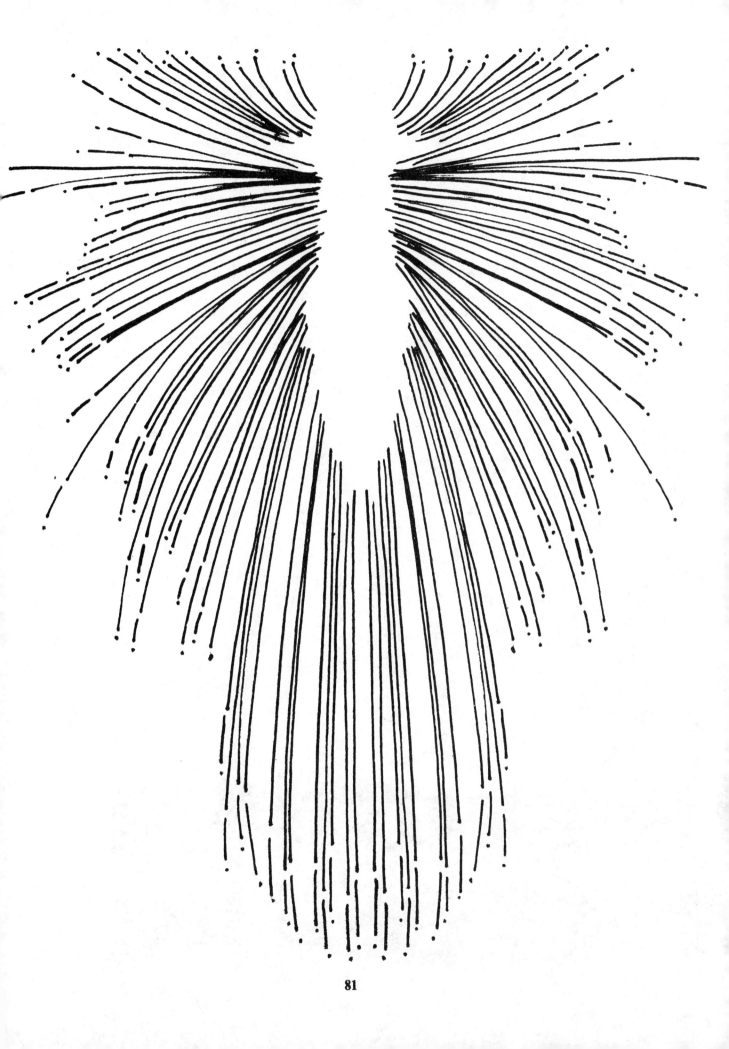

# Parting

Opening Meditation

*Leader* Lord, it is so difficult for us to say good-bye. It is hard to let go of people who have been very special to us, who have added so much to our lives. It is so risky to begin in a new direction, to begin our lives again. It is somewhat painful when we realize that what has been will now be sweet memories of what our lives once were.

*Reader* Luke 10:3-9, 16.

Silent Reflection

*All* And yet, our new beginnings will bring new growth, new awareness, and new people with whom we can share your love and your life. New adventures await us, Lord. May our goings and comings be blessed by your presence.

*Reader* Psalm 23

Silent Reflection

*Leader* Let us pray.

Spontaneous Prayer

*Leader* May the peace of the Lord be with us all.

*All* May his love be ever-present in our lives.

*Leader* Let us turn to one another and share a sign of the peace and love we have known.

*Leader* In the spirit of our union, let us together pray.

*All* Our Father . . .

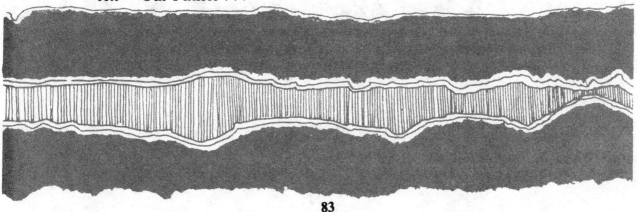

# *Leave-Taking*

OPENING MEDITATION

*Leader*    Let us pray. Father, as we bring a close to our gathering we are thankful for your presence among us. May we, in gratitude, go forth and make your way known to all those we meet. May your love and peace be evident in our lives. We ask this through our Lord, Jesus Christ. Amen.

*Reader*    Matthew 28:18-20

*Psalm Response*

*Left*    I will bless Yahweh at all times,
his praise shall be on my lips continually;
my soul glories in Yahweh,
let the humble hear and rejoice.

*Right*    Proclaim with me the greatness of Yahweh,
together let us extol his name.
I seek Yahweh, and he answers me
and frees me from all my fears.

*Left*    Every face turned to him grows brighter
and is never ashamed.

A cry goes up from the poor man, and Yahweh hears,
and helps him in all his troubles.

*Right*   How good Yahweh is—only taste and see!
Happy the man who takes shelter in him.
Fear Yahweh, you his holy ones:
those who fear him want for nothing.   *from Psalm 34*

SILENT REFLECTION

*Leader*   Let us pray.

SPONTANEOUS PRAYER

*Leader*   Father, hear our needs and remain with us as we go forth among
your people.

*All*   The Lord bless and keep you!
The Lord let his face shine upon you and be gracious to you!
The Lord look upon you kindly and give you peace.

*Leader*   Let us go in peace to love and serve the Lord.

*All*   Thanks be to God who sends us forth.

As We Go Forth

# As We Go Forth

**Leader**  Let us pray. Father, we go forth from this gathering renewed by your love and your word. We have been blessed by your presence in this assembly of your people. Be with us as we continue the work we have begun as we go out among others. Be our strength, our hope, our love and our life. We ask this through Jesus Christ, our Lord and brother. Amen.

**Reader**  Philippians 1:3-11

**All**  Lord, let our lives be rich with your love and the love of your people. Let us be constant in our affection for you. May our understanding of you always grow as we sing your glory and praise.

**Reader**  John 15:9-17

SILENT REFLECTION

**Reader**  As a celebrating people of our God, let us join together saying . . .

**All**  Our Father in heaven,
may your name be held holy,
your kingdom come,
your will be done
on earth as in heaven.
Give us today our daily bread.
And forgive us our debts,
as we have forgiven those who are in debt to us.
And do not put us to the test,
but save us from the evil one.

**Leader**  May he who is Lord give us continued peace in the days to come.

**All**  Amen.

**Leader**  May the grace of our Lord Jesus Christ be with you all.

**All**  And also with you.

# Resources

## Other Prayer Services

**Gathering Prayers**
Debra Hintz
These 35 Scripture-based services are appropriate for staff and faculty meetings, and all types of church gatherings.
0-89622-2969, 8 1/2 x 11, 80 pp., B-31, $7.95

**Prayer Services for Religious Educators**
Gwen Costello
Complete prayer experiences in a brief, accessible style for critical groups involved in faith-sharing.
0-89622-390-6, 8 1/2 x 11, 80 pp., W-93, $9.95

**Life-Cycle Celebrations for Women**
Marge Sears
This meaningful book encourages women to share, through celebration of ritual, their life experiences with those of others. Includes instructions for preparing each prayer service.
0-89622-399-x, 8 1/2 x 11, 88 pp., W-96, $9.95

**The Silver Lining**
**11 Personalized Scriptural Wake Services**
Dr. J. Massyngbaerde Ford
Consoling Scripture readings with original prayers attuned to the circumstances surrounding the death. Beautifully hard-bound, 2 ribbons.
0-89622-331-0, 6 x 9, 112 pp., W-21, $19.95

**Women's Prayer Services**
edited by Iben Gjerding & Katherine Kinnamon
A sharing of the ways women in their various contexts, alone and in community, express their faith through worship. Transcultural, ecumenical.
0-89622-329-9, 8 1/2 x 11, 80 pp., B-82, $7.95

**To order:**
Order directly from Twenty-Third Publications, P.O. Box 180, Mystic, CT 06355 or call toll-free 1-800-321-0411.